Your Retirement

How to Prepare for It
How to Enjoy It

A Comprehensive Guide for
Federal & Postal Employees and Retirees
From the Editors of the
Weekly Federal Employees' News Digest

By Bill Olcheski

Published 1991 by
Federal Employees' News Digest, Inc.
Post Office Box 7528
Falls Church, Virginia 22040-7528

Telephone (703) 533-3031

Printed in the United States of America

ISBN 0-910582-11-4

With thanks to my wife, children and grandchildren who proved to me that there is indeed life after retirement.

TABLE OF CONTENTS

FOREWORD

Most of us know we want to retire someday. But how to do it is another matter. When it comes time to "put in our papers," most of us have only a vague idea of what lies ahead, let alone what preparations we must make to give us a better chance of actually enjoying our "leisure" years.

One of the best ways to prepare for that day when we walk out of the office for the last time is to get our thinking straight about retirement itself, how to plan it, how to choose a retirement location and so on. We sent the highly-regarded veteran reporter/editor/consultant Bill Olcheski, president of Olcheski Enterprises of Falls Church, Virginia, himself a recent federal retiree, to the Office of Personnel Management, the Social Security Administration and other agencies dealing with federal and postal retirement to find out the essentials of what has become one of the largest and most complex retirement systems in the world. He spent hours upon hours interviewing the experts. He also spoke with recent and longtime retirees and their spouses to discover what difficulties they had and what advice they had to offer people facing retirement decisions and those who in retirement want to improve their situation. His and our sincere thanks to all of them, including OPM, SSA and the Federal Retirement Thrift Investment Board.

He found that without a blueprint, retirement can be a frightening prospect for many. A lack of preparation is the primary cause of an unsuccessful or a difficult move from active service to federal or postal retirement. And, Olcheski found that there is a very good reason why many federal and postal employees are confused and frustrated as they approach their "golden" years. There is no central source for retirement information for them. There are various government pamphlets and a labyrinth of official regulations to search through. There are seminars sponsored by federal agencies, and there are employees whose primary job is to help retirees decide what choices they must make to achieve a happy and secure retirement.

But before *Your Retirement: How to Prepare for It / How to Enjoy It* there was no one-stop source of answers to the kinds of questions that federal and postal employees ask when facing one of the biggest events in their lives—retirement.

As publishers of federal and postal employee news, including the *Weekly Federal Employees News Digest* and the *Federal Employees Almanac*, for more than 35 years, we take great pride in adding *Your Retirement* to our list of titles. For years we have been asked to create a book just like this one. Those of you who approached us emphasized that you did not want a "textbook," nor did you want a publication loaded with obscure language and technical jargon. And, you didn't want just bare facts or vague generalities. While this book won't answer every question you might have (it cannot possibly cover each and every special circumstance) we believe it will point you in the right direction by helping to orient your thinking. Where specifics were needed, we provided them.

What you wanted is a common sense explanation of what you are up against and some general advice on your retirement from an "informed friend." Made good sense to us.

To you we proudly dedicate this book.

Don Mace
Joseph Young
Eric Yoder
Editors

INTRODUCTION

Deciding to retire is one of the most important decisions you will make in your lifetime. It ranks up there with picking a mate, selecting a career or buying a house. If your retirement decision is the right one you can enjoy happy and productive years of retirement. Guess wrong and you have a blueprint for a miserable existence.

Is there life after retirement? You can bet there is! But you have to plan ahead and weigh all options before you are able to make informed decisions about retirement. You must understand your role and that of the government, and you have to be sure both are moving in the same direction.

In this book we deal primarily with voluntary retirement of employees of the federal government, including postal workers. While some of the subjects covered also will be of interest to those who retire involuntarily, our focus will be on those employees who have decided the time has come to "hang it up."

Your friends probably will advise you against retiring. They will tell you that the reduction in income will be catastrophic; that you will miss the day-to-day contact with your fellow employees, and that you will be bored stiff trying to find a use for all of the extra spare time you will have. Most of these warnings deal with situations that can be avoided.

In the chapters that follow we will explore many of the problems encountered by retirees. We will show you how to figure out how much money you will need in retirement. We then will show you how to determine the money you will have available to you and suggest ways to make up the difference if you have a shortfall. There will be chapters on how to select the area to which you want to retire and the steps you should take before making the move. We will give you guidance on determining whether to sell or keep your house if you decide to move to another part of the country.

There's an old song that notes "It Takes Two to Tango." For the married federal employee this means the needs and wishes of the spouse must be an integral part of the retirement plan. This book examines some of the problems you could be facing and suggests possible solutions.

In the months before retirement you will be bombarded with official directives about retirement. You should read all of them carefully, although most of you won't. We have done the reading for you and present key features in clear and concise language. Where tables are appropriate in explaining the subject matter we have provided them.

> *"Looking over the potential problems may make retirement seem like a dangerous road on which to embark."*

We also take a look at the Thrift Savings Plan, tell you who is eligible, how much can be deposited and what happens to the money when you retire.

Most of the material in this book deals with the CSRS and FERS retirement systems which cover the vast majority of federal and postal workers. We recognize that there are separate systems covering certain categories of employees, such as those in the Foreign Service. Most of the considerations covered apply equally as well to the other systems, but employees under them should make sure they gather the needed material from their agencies that will explain the differences.

It is important to remember that advice given in this book—or any other book for that matter—has to deal with generic answers to questions faced by most retirees. Questions dealing with a specific case should be answered by government officials familiar with the case. You cannot safely apply the answers someone else got to a specific situation just because your problems appear to be similar. Attempting to do so is not only foolhardy, it is dangerous. It is like taking someone else's medicine because their symptoms are similar to yours.

In the medical situation you could end up very dead. In the case of retirement you could find yourself financially ruined.

Rules change, and the ones that affected your friend might no longer apply to you. Congress spends a great deal of time fiddling with retirement programs. Luckily there are retiree organizations and sharp-eyed reporters working to keep you informed. Make use of them to keep up-to-date on the rules as they apply to you.

Looking over the potential problems may make retirement seem like a dangerous road on which to embark. While you have to be sensible, it is important to remember that retirement can be a wonderful time in your life. You and your spouse can travel or stay at home, garden or take healthful walks to the vegetable stand, sleep late in the mornings and just roll over when the radio announcer begins reeling off school and office closings due to bad weather.

You are able to make dental and doctor appointments during the day instead of having to take sick leave or skip your lunch to keep an appointment. You can take your spouse to a movie in the afternoon, see a first-run picture and pay only a fraction of the evening price for tickets. The same is true of having lunch at a nice restaurant. You can do it for much less than the same place charges in the evening.

You can dress more comfortably and casually and face life with a relaxed attitude. You can even go to a baseball game in the afternoon without needing to tell your boss that you had to visit a sick friend.

Our effort in this book is to handle some heavy subjects with a light hand. Before you get into the text, we offer for your consideration a list of the ten smartest things and the ten biggest mistakes you can make as you plan your retirement. Consider them carefully, they can make a big difference in whether you will enjoy retirement or live to regret your decision.

10 SMARTEST THINGS YOU CAN DO
AS YOU APPROACH RETIREMENT

1. Begin your retirement planning at least a year before you actually retire.

2. Attend a pre-retirement seminar the first time you are eligible. This will give you a basic framework on which to determine what type retirement you want, when you want it and how you will pay for it.

3. Keep your retirement plans confidential. This allows you to change your mind if retirement plans change.

4. Discuss your decision and plans with your spouse. Be sure that the interests of both will be preserved in your new lifestyle.

5. Be aware of the various retirement options. Discuss those options with the retirement counselor in your agency. Base your decision on facts, not on the advice of a friend who may have an entirely different situation.

6. Review your life and health insurance needs and figure the costs as you decide which policies to take with you into retirement.

7. Don't relocate for about a year after you retire. This will help you make a wise decision on whether you want to stay close to family and friends or move to a new area.

8. Take advantage of the various "thrift" plans available to you. Save the maximum you can even if you will only be in the program for a year or less.

9. Take a financial inventory. Verify all income sources available to you in retirement. See if you qualify for Social Security or other benefits. Review your investments for the highest possible return with the least risks. Budget for the unexpected expenses like increasing college tuition for your children or medical care for you or a loved one.

10. Read and review all retirement information provided by your agency and OPM. Be aware of help and advice available from retiree groups and organizations. Take advantage of that help.

10 BIGGEST MISTAKES YOU CAN MAKE AS YOU APPROACH RETIREMENT

1. Decide to retire on the spur of the moment because of some difficult assignment or personality clash on the job.

2. Decide to retire without discussing your plans with your spouse. You need the emotional support of your spouse when you make the decision that will change both of your lives.

3. Retire without having something to "retire to" as well as to "retire from." The lure of the fishing pond or the old rocking chair grows dull fast when you have nothing better to do.

4. Retire with the belief that you can live comfortably on your annuity without realistically comparing the money you will have coming in with the amount you will need to maintain your standard of living.

5. Failing to stay abreast of developments and changes in federal retirement entitlements and trends.

6. Retire without reviewing all of the retirement options and understanding the pros and cons of each.

7. Base retirement decisions on the advice of friends rather than consulting the experts.

8. Selling your house and moving to a strange area without visiting the area before making a permanent change. Failing to consider renting for about a year to be sure the new area offers the cultural, social and economic advantages you are seeking.

9. Believing that your active, productive life is over just because you are retiring.

10. Failing to review all of your service and entitlements to be sure you get proper credit.

Source: Office of Personnel Management

DISTRIBUTION BY AGE OF EMPLOYEE AND SURVIVOR ANNUITANTS ON THE RETIREMENT ROLL AT THE END OF FISCAL YEAR 1988

	Employee Annuitants								Survivor Annuitants							
	Nondisability Retirements				Disability Retirements				Adults				Children			
	On Roll		Monthly Annuity		On Roll		Monthly Annuity		On Roll		Monthly Annuity		On Roll		Monthly Annuity	
Age Category	Number	Percent	Mean	Median	Number	Percent	Mean	Median	Number	Percent	Mean	Median	Number	Percent	Mean	Median
Under 19									20	0.0	601	435	25,859	61.2	241	245
19–22	2	0.0	204	204	93	0.0	555	509	22	0.0	542	471	6,503	15.4	247	245
23–29	105	0.0	992	913	869	0.3	613	604	245	0.0	405	370	1,617	3.8	245	244
30–34	2,411	0.2	1,133	1,038	3,566	1.1	667	655	961	0.2	401	370	1,641	3.9	247	244
35–39	17,029	1.4	1,459	1,342	7,454	2.4	742	707	2,423	0.5	450	404	1,608	3.8	252	244
40–44	97,534	7.9	1,535	1,404	10,250	3.3	797	750	4,339	0.9	503	438	1,339	3.2	257	244
45–49	231,053	18.7	1,330	1,216	18,777	5.8	856	780	7,918	1.6	545	462	943	2.2	263	245
50–54	325,704	26.3	1,229	1,129	34,777	11.2	886	799	15,526	3.1	566	485	795	1.9	268	246
55–59	254,014	20.5	1,248	1,129	59,196	19.0	937	831	31,645	6.3	589	516	649	1.5	271	292
60–64	159,462	12.9	1,237	1,110	75,920	24.4	1,025	886	62,553	12.5	619	542	645	1.5	274	293
65–69	89,825	7.3	1,160	1,022	53,562	17.2	995	862	86,572	17.4	642	557	412	1.0	278	294
70–74	40,379	3.3	1,015	895	28,964	9.3	904	780	86,474	17.3	653	564	151	0.4	285	296
75–79	16,143	1.3	896	805	11,840	3.8	806	701	78,722	15.8	644	554	56	0.1	286	296
80–84	3,124	0.3	761	650	4,454	1.4	665	586	60,941	12.2	602	516	21	0.0	265	292
85–89	315	0.0	694	612	1,891	0.6	603	538	39,284	7.9	544	477	1	0.0	296	296
90–94					297	0.1	510	426	16,473	3.3	499	459				
95–99					21	0.0	547	420	3,568	0.7	440	380				
100 and over									734	0.1	500	415				
Age Unknown									305	0.1	262	343				
TOTAL	1,237,100	100.0	1,262	1,157	311,263	100.0	930	810	498,725	100.0	612	525	42,240	100.0	246	245
62 and over	1,051,533	85.0	1,223	1,113	216,537	69.6	964	837	414,406	83.1	620	535	1,001	2.4	279	294
65 and over	888,966	71.9	1,211	1,098	176,949	56.8	967	837	372,768	74.7	620	535	641	1.5	280	296
Mean Age	69.5				65.2				71.4				21.4			
Median Age	69				66				72				17			

CHAPTER 1
A LOOK AT THE CALENDAR

When is the best time to begin planning for your retirement?
Yesterday!

If you have already missed the deadline start today, regardless of the amount of time you have left before you are eligible to retire.

Begin by gathering up all of the papers you have that deal with your civil service career and actions that would affect that career. Start a "working" file which will document all changes in your status during your career.

In the file put your birth certificate, records of your military service, military separation papers, records of any part-time government service, and even records of service which you you are not sure will count toward your retirement. There are circumstances under which service as a consultant or a contract employee qualifies for such credit. You will need all of the documentation to insure proper credit is received.

Keep your employment record in the file. Update it periodically to adequately reflect your service time and grades in which such service was performed.

If you are still working for the government, your personnel office can be of great help to you. Ask to see your personnel folder. Be sure the personal file you are maintaining matches the material in the official folder.

If you find documents in the official folder that you do not have in your personal file, make copies of them so that your file will be complete. Remember that your agency closes your file and sends the contents to a records center shortly after you retire. It is much easier to gather the material while it is still available close at hand rather than trying to retrieve it later.

As you get closer to the actual retirement date you will be taking more concrete steps. A word of caution before going into detail. Don't feel you have to tell the world when you set a tentative retirement date. The only office that really needs to know is the personnel office and it is required to keep the information confidential.

Spreading the word too quickly can jeopardize your chances of advancement in your current job. It also could encourage your supervisor to begin thinking in terms of shifting your responsibilities to someone else. This is OK if you actually retire on the tentative date set. However, should you change your mind, you may find you have burned too many bridges behind you.

Remember that you can change your mind up until the last minute. An agency must permit a voluntary retiree to withdraw his or her application at any time before the effective date of separation.

If you are in an agency where "early outs" are programmed and you are one of the candidates, you have exactly the same rights you would have if you retired at the normal time.

The only difference is that you would be operating on a compressed time schedule. Make a quick study of the information presented in this book and in material provided by your personnel office. You probably will be getting a smaller annuity because of your early departure. That's another major reason for being aware of all your rights and how to protect them.

Many agencies have pre-retirement seminars. They usually are scheduled once or twice a year. Generally persons who need less than five years to qualify for retirement are eligible to attend. Attending such a seminar does not commit you to a specified retirement time. It is a good idea to attend the first one for which you are eligible. You will be given a good idea of the decisions you will have to make at retirement time. You will have time to weigh the various options at your leisure and thus make better judgments based on your awareness of the facts. Remember the old saying that decisions made in haste are repented at leisure. Give yourself all of the time you need to research the options and then decide.

When you are within about a year of your planned retirement

time you should make an appointment with a retirement counselor, probably in the personnel office, to review your official records. It is at such a meeting that you should make a record of all the service listed for you, identifying the agencies and the dates during which you served.

Make sure your official records include effective dates for adjustments to your pay or tour of duty. Also at this time review the current designation of beneficiary for your life insurance.

Health benefits and life insurance coverage also should be evaluated. You need to know the benefits you will carry with you into retirement and which will be lost. It is important to know that there are restrictions on continuing your benefits after retirement. Generally, if you were not enrolled in the plans for the five years preceding your retirement you cannot continue your life insurance or health benefits into retirement. Federal health benefits coverage as a family member counts toward the five-year requirement. For more details on carrying over health or life insurance into retirement, see chapter 4.

As you review your folder verify that your age and date of birth are listed correctly. If somewhere back along the line you fudged on the date for whatever reason, now is the time to 'fess up. You might get away with fibbing about your age to a spouse, but for either civil service retirement or Social Security benefits you must have proof of your date of birth and hence your true age.

If any of the documents in your file are incomplete or incorrect, take steps to correct the errors immediately. Any discrepancies could result in loss of benefits, or at least a delay in receipt of the benefits if the documentation is incomplete.

The meeting with the counselor is the time to request estimated annuity payments and factors which could change the amount of the payments. You may have to make a deposit in order to have certain service count toward your retirement.

Three situations in which you may want to make a deposit involve:

- Military service after 1956.
- Federal service for which no retirement deductions were withheld.

- Federal service for which you have received a refund of retirement deductions. This would not apply if you received the refund for service subject to the Federal Employees Retirement System (FERS).

Deposits covering military service after 1956 must be made to your agency before you retire if the time is to count toward your retirement.

All of these decisions can be delayed until you are about five months from retirement. However, the sooner you know the approximate amount of your annuity the sooner you can decide if you want to make the deposits. They can be hefty.

If you already are receiving retirement pay for military service, such service will not be creditable toward your civil service retirement. But, it is possible to waive your military retirement pay in order to receive credit for your military service. If you elect to do so, write to your Military Finance Center at least three months before your planned retirement date. Check with your personnel office for the location of the center nearest to you. Your personnel officer can advise you on selecting the date on which you want the waiver to be effective. To complete the waiver you will need to submit a copy of your waiver request and any response you have received from the Military Finance Center. Copies of these, as well as all other pertinent papers, should be included in your personal file.

When you are within about four months of retirement you should contact your personnel office for the necessary retirement forms. By getting the forms this far in advance you will have time to review them and learn if you need to acquire any documentation or support papers. Getting ready for retirement is like the countdown for a missile launch. Remember that you can stop the process at any point until you submit the retirement request. Changes may occur in your agency or in your job that will change your decision. That is why your date should be kept confidential as long as possible.

Shortly before "lift off" time submit the retirement application and related forms to your supervisor, being sure to keep a copy for your own records. You now move into "lame duck" status and the final countdown for your departure begins. Your friends begin preparing some cute cards for you and your supervisor begins a search for your replacement.

Both your agency and the U.S. Office of Personnel Management have important roles to play in processing your retirement application.

The processing begins in the personnel office at your agency. Your personnel records will be checked to insure that you have the necessary age and service requirements to qualify for retirement. They also will determine your right to continue your government insurance coverage. You will be given a summary of your government service and will be asked to certify that the information is complete and correct.

Your agency also will:

- Verify your coverage under the group life insurance program and then certify your right to continue this coverage to the U.S. Office of Personnel Management (OPM).

- Transfer your federal health benefits enrollment to OPM once eligibility is established.

- Process the personnel papers necessary to separate you from the service.

- Forward your application and pertinent records to your agency's payroll office.

The payroll office will authorize your final salary payment and a lump-sum payment for any accrued annual leave you have. You will be paid for all of the leave, even if the total exceeds any "use or lose" leave. However, if you plan to retire early in the new year, you could lose any accrued leave you would normally have been required to take during the preceding calendar year. Check the exact status of your leave with your personnel office.

If you are retiring in the middle of a pay period, be sure your administrative officer has submitted a time and attendance sheet to cover the partial payment due you. Failure to do so could result in the need to reopen your records and thus would delay receipt of your first retirement check.

The payroll office then will certify and close out your records. The official record of your service is now complete. It shows your retirement contributions for your current service, pay rates, unused sick leave credit for retirement purposes, last day of pay and the date and type of separation. This information will be used by OPM to determine your retirement benefits. The completed package then is put on a "Register of Separations and Transfers" to OPM, Employee Service and Records Center, Boyers, Pennsylvania 16017.

The action taken by the payroll office will be the last opportunity your agency will have to handle your records.

"Under OPM's current standards, your agency is expected to complete its personnel office and payroll office processing actions within 30 days after you separate."

Under OPM's current standards, your agency is expected to complete its personnel office and payroll office processing actions within 30 days after you separate.

If you are separating under a disability retirement your application will receive different processing. Your agency will send your application, evidence supporting your disability claim and preliminary retirement records to OPM. OPM will review the records and determine if you qualify for disability retirement. If you are eligible OPM will notify your agency to separate you from its rolls.

You will know when your application has been received by OPM because you will receive a claim number. This number begins with the letters "CSA." All retirees will be given the "CSA" number even if they retire under FERS. It is important to keep this number handy as you will need to refer to it every time you contact OPM about your claim.

The only time the number changes is upon the death of a retiree. At that time the number is preceded by CSF which means Civil Service Final.

The Employee Service and Records Center will review your

retirement papers and any records OPM may have of your service in agencies other than the one from which you retired.

Once your entitlement to an annuity is clear OPM will authorize interim payments to provide you with an income until your claim is completed. These payments usually are about 85 percent of what your regular monthly payment will be. Payments usually are authorized within two weeks after OPM receives your retirement package from your personnel office. It takes the Treasury Department about another week to process your check. The Postal Service takes a few more days to deliver it. Thus, you should receive your first check about four weeks after you retire. You will receive a notice ahead of time telling you the amount to expect.

After the Employee Service and Records Center completes its action your claim will go to the OPM Office of Retirement Programs in Washington. Your claim will be assigned to an examiner for final adjudication. He or she will check all the records and contact you if any information is missing.

If you are found eligible to elect an alternative annuity (that is, a reduced monthly annuity with a lump-sum payment of your retirement contributions), the claims examiner will determine the amount of your monthly benefit under both the regular and alternative annuity provisions of the retirement law. He or she will then send you information about this benefit in addition to specific tax information relating to your annuity. You will have 30 days in which to decide if you want to exercise the lump-sum option.

OPM should be able to complete the final adjudication of fully documented claims within 60 to 65 days from the date it receives your retirement package from the individual payroll offices. The amount of time it takes to complete the processing will vary with the complexity of your case. One consolation is that the interim payments will continue until the processing is complete. At that time you will receive an adjusted check representing the difference between what you received in the interim payments and the amount actually due.

Alternative annuities, providing for lump-sum payment of contributions to the retirement fund, are discussed in chapter 2.

PRE-RETIREMENT CHECK LIST

❑ Determine a tentative retirement date.

❑ Determine if you are eligible for disability or other special type of retirement.

❑ Start a career file of important papers. These should include birth certificate, marriage license, military discharges and any official notices relating to personnel actions.

❑ List dates and documentation for all federal government service including full and part-time positions.

❑ Compare your list with your personnel file to insure accuracy of your records and proper credit for your service.

❑ Update your Form 171. It will be the basis for your resume if you seek employment after you retire.

❑ Sign up for pre-retirement seminar at your agency.

❑ Meet with retirement counselor in your agency to check eligibility and get preliminary figures on annuity.

❑ Decide whether you want to continue your life and health insurance policies. Verify cost of doing so.

❑ Complete all necessary retirement forms.

❑ Submit retirement application to your supervisor.

CHAPTER 2
RETIREMENT OPTIONS

Retirement options for federal employees fall into four general categories: voluntary, deferred, disability and involuntary.

Voluntary retirement is based on a combination of age and years of service. It has two major requirements:

- You must have completed at least five years of federal civilian service and,

- You must have been employed under the Civil Service Retirement System (CSRS) or the Federal Employees Retirement System (FERS) for at least one of the last two years of your federal service. You also must have been contributing to the retirement fund during the last year.

The amount of service you need to qualify for retirement goes down as you get older. For instance, you can retire at age 55 if you have 30 years of service. At age 60 you need 20 years of service; and, at age 62, you need only five years.

Special provisions govern the voluntary retirement of law enforcement officers and firefighters, as well as air traffic controllers. The former can retire at age 50 with 20 years of service. The latter can retire at age 50 after 20 years as an air traffic controller or at any age with 25 years service in air traffic control.

There are some circumstances under which you might want to apply for a deferred retirement. Suppose that, at age 48, you qualified for retirement based on years of service and decided to leave the civil service for a career in the private sector. Rather than take a reduced annuity, you could leave your deposits in the retirement fund until you became 62. About two months before becoming 62 you could submit your retirement application to OPM and your annuity would begin at age 62. It is important to remember that your former agency will no longer have your records so the application would have to be made to OPM.

Disability retirements are granted to federal and postal workers covered by CSRS or FERS who become unable to continue in their jobs because of a disabling condition.

An employee must meet all of the following conditions to be eligible for disability retirement:

- Have completed at least five years of federal service under CSRS or 18 months under FERS.

- The disability must have occurred while in a job subject to the retirement system. You must be totally disabled for useful and efficient service in your current job, or any other vacant position of the same grade or pay level. Before an employee is determined to be disabled, it must be demonstrated that he or she is not qualified for reassignment within the agency. OPM emphasizes that disability retirement is a "last resort," appropriate only when every reasonable effort to preserve the person's employment has failed.

- The application for disability retirement must be filed with OPM by the employee. The only exceptions are situations in which neither the employee nor a member of his or her immediate family is able to make the application; or, if the employee is mentally incompetent to complete the application.

If the application is made by the agency, it must be filed with OPM before the employee is separated from the service. If application is made by the employee or designated alternate it must be filed within one year after separation from the service. Employees who are covered both by CSRS or FERS and Social Security, should submit disability retirement applications to both OPM and the Social Security office.

Involuntary separations or early retirements sometimes occur because of a lack of funds resulting in a reduction-in-force; inefficiency (unless due to employee's misconduct); disability (provided the separation is initiated by the agency), and separation during probation because of failure to qualify. Under CSRS, if the retiring employee is under age 55 the basic life annuity rate is permanently reduced by 1/6 of 1 percent for each full month (2 percent per year) that he or she is under age 55. Under FERS, benefits are not reduced for employees retiring under involuntary separation rules. However, the annuity is not payable if the worker retires before the minimum retirement age.

A reduction-in-force (RIF) allows early retirement of qualified employees who have at least 25 years of service or who have at least 20 years service at age 50. Such retirements may be made voluntarily during a period when the employing agency is undergoing a major RIF, a reorganization, or transfer of function. The RIF must be expected to force separation of or an immediate pay reduction for a significant number of employees in the agency.

If an employee resigns after receiving a notice of separation because his or her job is abolished or the agency is liquidated, such separation is considered involuntary for retirement purposes.

Some employees may be offered another position, demotion or reassignment in lieu of separation. If the offered position is no lower than two grades below an employee's current position, it must be accepted or the retirement will be considered voluntary.

In all discussions of length of service required for retirement we encounter the term "creditable civil service." There are three tests to determine if time served in a given job can be counted as federal service:

- The employee must be engaged in the performance of federal duties.

- He or she must have been appointed by a federal officer.

- Work must have been performed under the supervision and direction of a federal officer.

The type of appointment is immaterial in determining if service can be counted toward retirement eligibility. However, pay must have been received for the service. Service in the Executive, Legislative and Judicial branches of the federal government and the District of Columbia can be counted. Service performed under other federal contributory retirement systems is creditable if contributions were refunded and deposited to the Civil Service Retirement Fund.

Time spent in the military can be counted toward retirement eligibility. Only honorable service is counted. The applicant must not be receiving retirement or other pay from the military unless it is for a service-connected disability incurred in combat or in line of duty during wartime. Service can be counted for time spent in any branch of the armed forces, the regular or reserve corps of the Public Health Service, or as a commissioned officer of the National Oceanic & Atmospheric Administration. Also countable is service performed in reserve components of the armed forces while on active duty or active duty for training.

Once you have identified your creditable service you then have to compute how much time you have served toward your retirement eligibility. Your personnel office already will have done this computation to arrive at your Service Computation Date. Be sure your records arrive at the same conclusion as those in your official file. If they do not, compare the records and make necessary adjustments.

These are the general rules for computing the time you have accumulated toward your retirement eligibility:

- Federal civilian service counts from the day of appointment to the last day of work. If you have a break in service during your government career, stop counting when the break begins and resume when it ends.

- Military time counts from the date of entry on active duty to the discharge or separation date.

- You cannot count your military time if you are receiving retirement pay as a result of your military service. An exception to this rule is made when the retirement pay you are receiving from the military is based on a disability discharge resulting from injuries in war time.

- Military service after 1956 can only be counted if a deposit is made to cover the military time. Your personnel office will compute the deposit you will have to make in order to be able to count the military service.

Employees covered under FERS may have military service treated as a service credit under that program only if they pay 3 percent of the basic pay earned through that military service.

It also is possible to receive credit under CSRS or FERS for service for which no retirement deductions were made. However, a deposit must be made to cover the outstanding amounts plus applicable interest. The outstanding base amount is the deduction that would have been made to the respective system if deductions were made when the service was performed. In general, the circumstances that led to service being performed without deductions from pay being required were eliminated at the times FERS was enacted.

INTEREST CHARGES

Payments made to CSRS or FERS to capture or recapture service credit —including military, non-deduction, or service for which contributions were withdrawn—must be paid back with interest. The amount of interest charged varies depending on the time and circumstances of the contribution.

In most cases interest is charged at the following rates:

Years before 1984	3.00%
1985	13.00%
1986	11.10%
1987	9.00%
1988	9.40%
1989	9.10%
1990	8.75%
1991	8.625%

Exceptions to the above rates are: (1) non-deduction service earned before October 1, 1982, and redeposits of funds made before October 1, 1982. Interest of 3 percent is charged in all such cases. (2) In the case of military service, interest is only charged beginning two years after the beginning of civilian employment. In any event, interest is not charged for service before October 1985.

VOLUNTARY CONTRIBUTIONS

Employees covered by CSRS can increase their benefits by voluntary contributions to the Retirement Fund. Such deposits earn interest at the rate shown above.

Voluntary contributions may not exceed 10 percent of basic salary since August 1, 1920. The minimum voluntary contribution is $25. Additional contributions must be made in $25 increments. Payments may be made at any time and do not need to follow a fixed schedule. No voluntary contributions may be made unless contributions have been made to the Retirement Fund for all civilian service since August 1, 1920. If you want to make voluntary contributions you need to file Standard Form 2804 with OPM. Payments must be made directly to OPM.

If you die after retirement, your survivor will be paid an additional annuity equal to 50 percent of your reduced additional annuity. If the total annuity paid to you and your survivor is less than your voluntary contributions with interest, the difference will be payable as a lump-sum benefit. If you die before retirement, voluntary contributions, with interest, will be paid as a lump-sum death benefit. The voluntary contributions may not be used to provide additional annuity for your survivors.

Voluntary contributions may be refunded to you at any time before you draw any of the additional annuity that these contributions buy. Interest is paid on the contributions to the date of your refund or separation from service, whichever comes first.

If you elect to withdraw your contributions you must withdraw the total amount. Taking this option bans you from making voluntary contributions in future years. The only way you can get back into the program is by leaving federal or postal service and then being re-employed under the retirement system.

Standard Form SF 2802 is the form to use if you want to request refund of your voluntary contributions.

LUMP-SUM ANNUITY OPTION

Until 1991 the lump-sum alternative annuity—a payment equaling an individual's lifetime contributions to the retirement fund—was an entitlement that many retiring federal and postal employees eagerly took advantage of. But in 1990, Congress and the White House agreed to suspend the popular option until October 1, 1995 for most employees.

Now only those in the following groups may opt for the lump-sum payment:

- Workers who are "involuntarily separated," except specifically excluded from this category are Members of Congress, the Vice President, and political employees of the executive branch. Those who are eligible can receive a lump-sum payable in two installments of 50 percent each, one soon after retirement, the other a year later.

- Workers designated by the Department of Defense as essential to Operation Desert Shield, including members of reserve forces mobilized because of that Operation. Such individuals will have until December 1, 1991 to retire with the option for a lump-sum in 50/50 installments, provided they were eligible to retire as of December 1, 1990.

- Individuals eligible to voluntarily retire (not disability), and who are certified as having a life-threatening or certain other critical illness, can continue to exercise the lump-sum option, in one payment at retirement.

In all of these cases, the lump-sum will result in a reduction to monthly benefits. The reduction is complex, but is based on life-expectancy tables and assumptions about the future of the economy. In principle, the decision is intended to be financially neutral, although of course some individuals would be made better or worse off, either by taking the option or rejecting it.

RETIREMENT OPTIONS CHECK LIST

❑ Review retirement options: voluntary, deferred, disability and involuntary.

❑ Become familiar with age and service requirements of each type.

❑ Check to see if you qualify under special programs such as those for law enforcement, fire fighters and air traffic controllers.

❑ Determine if you qualify for early retirement under RIF or other special retirement programs.

❑ Be sure you understand "creditable service." If not, review rules outlined in this chapter. If you feel your situation has "special circumstances," consult with your personnel office.

CSRS/FERS BENEFITS AT A GLANCE

Provision	Civil Service Retirement System (CSRS)	Federal Employees Retirement System (FERS)
Basic Annuity: Retirement		
Basic plan design	Defined benefit	Defined benefit not "integrated," i.e., it is fully added to social security
Required employee contributions	7% of total pay plus 1.45% Medicare	Social Security tax, 7.65% plus 0.8 percent retirement
Vesting (retirement)	5 yrs. for retirement	Same as CSRS
Salary base	Avg. of high-3 yrs. salary	Same as CSRS
Retirement benefit formula (accrual rate)	1.5% x first 5 yrs. of service; 1.75% x second 5 yrs. of service; 2.0% x all yrs. of service	High 3 years average salary times 1%, times years of service, or 1.1% at age 62 with 20 years of service
Unreduced retirement benefits	Age 55 with 30 yrs. of service; age 60 with 20 yrs. of service; age 62 with 5 yrs. of service	Age 62 and 5 yrs. of service; age 60 and 20 yrs. of service; or "minimum retirement age" (MRA) MRA = 1987-2002, age 55; 2002-2008, increases 2 mos. per yr.; 2009-2020, age 56; 2021-2026, increases 2 mos. per yr.; 2027 and after, age 57.
Reduced retirement benefits	N/A	MRA and 10 yrs. of service. Reduced by 5% for yrs. under age 62
Optional (RIFs or reorganizations) or involuntary early retirement; age and reductions	Age 50 with 20 yrs. of service; any age with 25 yrs. of service. Benefit reduced 2.0% for each yr. under age 55	Unreduced benefits at age 50 with 20 yrs. of service; any age with 25 yrs. of service

Provision	Civil Service Retirement System (CSRS)	Federal Employees Retirement System (FERS)
Deferred retirement	At least 5 yrs. of service; accrued benefit payable at age 62	Unreduced benefit at age 62, if employee had 5 yrs. of civilian service at termination and did not get refund of contributions, or upon attaining the MRA and had 30 yrs. of service at separation, or is age 60 with 20 yrs. of service at separation. Reduced benefit available upon reaching the MRA to vested employee with 10 yrs. of service
Pre-62 supplement for early retirement	N/A	Payable at retirement (but no earlier than MRA) until age 62; approximately equal to projected social security benefit payable at age 62, attributable to Federal service Supplement is subject to earnings test, similar to the test used by social security at age 62, reducing supplement if retiree has earned income in excess of an annual exempt amount ($7,080 in 1991, wage-indexed)
Refunds	Option to withdraw sums contributed at separation with benefits forfeited, unless subsequently made redeposit	Option to withdraw contributions, plus interest, at separation with benefits irrevocably forfeited

Provision	Civil Service Retirement System (CSRS)	Federal Employees Retirement System (FERS)
Cost-of-living adjustments (COLAs)	Payable to all annuitants. Annually, full rate of inflation measured by CPI: 5.4% in 1991	Payable only to regular retirees over age 62, or disabled (after first yr.) and survivors at any age

Increase in CPI	Annual COLA percentage
up to 2%	Same as CPI increase
2% to 3%	2%
3%+.	CPI increase minus 1 percentage point

4.4% in 1991

Disability Benefits

Provision	Civil Service Retirement System (CSRS)	Federal Employees Retirement System (FERS)
Vesting (disability)	5 yrs. of service	18 mos. of service
Definition of disability	Unable to do own job or vacant position at same grade or pay level in same agency and commuting area	Same as CSRS
Disability benefit amounts	Annuity earned at onset, or if greater, the lower of (1) 40% of salary base, or (2) the annuity that would be paid projecting service to age 60 at the same salary base. Benefits increased annually by full CPI	For the first yr. of eligibility, 60% of high-3 pay minus 100% of any social security payable. After the first yr., 40% of high-3 pay minus 60% of any social security payable. No COLAs provided the first yr.; thereafter, COLAs provided on the same basis as for retirees aged 62 and over

Provision	Civil Service Retirement System (CSRS)	Federal Employees Retirement System (FERS)
Retirement benefits after disability	Disability pension continues for life if no recovery before normal retirement age	At age 62 the annuity will be re-computed. For the retirement recomputation, the period of disability would be credited toward yrs. of service, and average pay would be increased to reflec COLAs applicable during that period
Preretirement death benefit—spouse	At death of worker with at least 18 mos. of service, surviving spouse receives 55% of the accrued benefit, or, if larger, the lesser of (1) 55% of 40% of salary base, or (2) 55% of the accrued annuity with service projected to age 60 at same high-3	At death of worker with at least 18 mos. but less than 10 yrs. of service, the benefit is a one-time payment of $17,938 in 1991 plus one-half of the deceased worker's final annual pay. If the deceased worker had 10 or more yrs. of service, an annuity is also payable equal to 50% of the accrued annuity
Preretirement death benefit—children	Unrelated to annuity. Annually adjusted amount varies by number of children and whether or not orphaned. Children must be (1) unmarried, (2) under age 18 or 22 if in school, or (3) any age and incapable of self-support if disability started before age 18	The amount in excess, if any, of payments to children under CSRS (to all children in family) over the children's social security benefits

Provision	Civil Service Retirement System (CSRS)	Federal Employees Retirement System (FERS)
Postretirement death benefit—spouse	Annuity to married retiree automatically reduced by 2.5% of first $300 monthly plus 10% of remainder unless jointly waived, but raised to unreduced level after death or divorce of spouse (unless otherwise stipulated in a divorce decree).*	Annuity to retiree reduced by 10% (or 5% if lower benefit is jointly elected) to provide a survivor annuity, unless jointly waived, but raised to unreduced level after death or divorce of the spouse, unless otherwise stipulated in a divorce decree
	Benefit equal to 55% of the annuity received by the retiree at the time of death, excluding the reduction for survivor election and including any reduction for involuntary early retirement. No social security for Federal employment	If the survivor is under age 60 and social security survivor benefits are **not** payable, benefits are lesser of (1) current CSRS or (2) 50% (25% if elected) of accrued annuity plus a social security "equivalent." When social security survivor benefits are payable, FERS pays 50% (25% if elected) of the deceased retiree's annuity
Postretirement death benefits—children	Same as preretirement death	Same as preretirement death

* Pertains to retirements and divorces occurring after May 6, 1985

TREND: 75-YEAR FUNDING PROJECTION – CSRS AND FERS COMBINED

Income and Benefit Outlays as a Percentage of Total Payroll

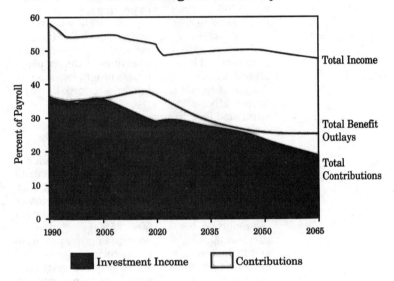

Fund Balance as a Percentage of Total Payroll

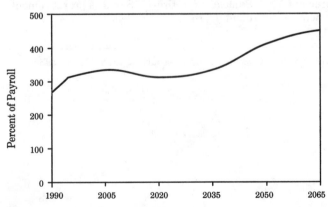

CHAPTER 3
DOLLARS AND SENSE

THE INCOME

All employees retiring in the future will receive an annuity which will be based on either the Civil Service Retirement System, the Federal Employees Retirement System or a combination of the two. The various parts of the retirement payments are referred to as "components".

Every employee who retires under FERS with one month or more of FERS service will have a FERS component. To have a CSRS component the employee must have:

- voluntarily **elected** to join FERS and,
- had at least five years creditable service, normally under Social Security or CSRS at the time the employee came into FERS.

CREDITING OF SERVICE

FERS Component. Consists of four categories:

- Service during which only FERS deductions were withheld.
- Service during which both Social Security and CSRS deductions were withheld.
- Military service performed **after** first coming under FERS.
- Service covered only by Social Security and performed after coming under FERS **and** before January 1, 1989, under which a deposit for it was either paid or deemed paid.

CSRS Component. Consists of four categories

- Service during which only CSRS deductions were withheld.
- Military service performed **before** first coming under FERS.
- Service covered only by Social Security and performed

before coming under FERS. (a deposit to the retirement fund is required before such service can be counted.)

- Unused sick leave.

CHART FOR CONVERTING UNUSED SICK LEAVE INTO INCREASED SERVICETIME CREDIT FOR HIGHER ANNUITIES (CSRS EMPLOYEES ONLY)*

No. of Days	1 Day & Up	1 Mo. & Up	2 Mo. & Up	3 Mo. & Up	4 Mo. & Up	5 Mo. & Up	6 Mo. & Up	7 Mo. & Up	8 Mo. & Up	9 Mo. & Up	10 Mo. & Up	11 Mo. & Up
0	—	174	348	522	696	870	1044	1217	1391	1565	1739	1913
1	6	180	354	528	701	875	1049	1223	1397	1571	1745	1919
2	12	186	359	533	707	881	1055	1229	1403	1577	1751	1925
3	17	191	365	539	713	887	1061	1235	1409	1583	1757	1930
4	23	197	371	545	719	893	1067	1241	1415	1588	1762	1936
5	29	203	377	551	725	899	1072	1246	1420	1594	1768	1942
6	35	209	383	557	730	904	1078	1252	1426	1600	1774	1948
7	41	214	388	562	736	910	1084	1258	1432	1606	1780	1954
8	46	220	394	568	742	916	1090	1264	1438	1612	1786	1959
9	52	226	400	574	748	922	1096	1270	1444	1617	1791	1965
10	58	232	406	580	754	928	1101	1275	1449	1623	1797	1971
11	64	238	412	586	759	933	1107	1281	1455	1629	1803	1977
12	70	243	417	591	765	939	1113	1287	1461	1635	1809	1983
13	75	249	423	597	771	945	1119	1293	1467	1641	1815	1958
14	81	255	429	603	777	951	1125	1299	1472	1646	1820	1994
15	87	261	435	609	783	957	1130	1304	1478	1652	1826	2000
16	93	267	441	615	788	962	1136	1310	1484	1658	1832	2006
17	99	272	446	620	794	968	1142	1316	1490	1664	1838	2012
18	104	278	452	626	800	974	1148	1322	1496	1670	1844	2017
19	110	284	458	632	806	980	1154	1328	1501	1675	1849	2023
20	116	290	464	638	812	986	1159	1333	1507	1681	1855	2029
21	122	296	470	643	817	991	1165	1339	1513	1687	1861	2035
22	128	301	475	649	823	997	1171	1345	1519	1693	1867	2041
23	133	307	481	655	829	1003	1177	1351	1525	1699	1873	2046
24	139	313	487	661	835	1009	1183	1357	1530	1704	1878	2052
25	145	319	493	667	841	1015	1188	1362	1536	1710	1884	2058
26	151	325	499	672	846	1020	1194	1368	1542	1716	1890	2064
27	157	330	504	678	852	1026	1200	1374	1548	1722	1896	2070
28	162	336	510	684	858	1032	1206	1380	1554	1728	1901	2075
29	168	342	516	690	864	1038	1212	1386	1559	1733	1907	2081

HOW TO USE THIS CHART — To find the increased service time credit for unused sick leave, use the following formula: find

***FERS employees may not convert unused sick leave for extra retirement credit.**

the number of hours of unused sick leave. In the horizontal column you will find the number of months and in the vertical column the remaining number of days. For example, 441 hours equals 2 months and 16 days. Another example: 1455 hours-equals 8 months and 11 days.

The annuity you will receive under either system is based on the average of your salary during the three highest consecutive years of your government employment. The salary figure used includes your regular pay, premium pay, and night differential for wage grade employees. It does not include bonuses, overtime or special allowances.

There are certain periods of federal service that do not count toward retirement. They include:

- Unpaid redeposit service. This would occur if you worked for the federal government for a few years and received a refund of your retirement deposits when you left. If you later came back into government, those deposits would have to be repaid before the time could count toward retirement.

- Civilian service after October 1, 1982 for which no deductions for retirement were taken from your salary and no deposit has been made.

- (NOTE: For FERS only). Remember that a person who withdraws his or her contributions on leaving government and then returns may not ever redeposit and get credit for that FERS service.

- Military service after 1956 for which no retirement deposit has been made if you were first hired in a position covered by CSRS or FERS on or after October 1, 1982.

- Military service after 1956 for which no deposit has been made if you were first hired in a position covered by CSRS or FERS before October 1, 1982, and eligible for Social Security benefits at retirement age (62 or over).

The amount of income you will have available to you in retirement is one of the major factors in deciding whether you are ready to retire. For many federal employees the monthly annuity check will be a major part of that income.

Due to major changes in the retirement system in recent years (the arrival of FERS, the development of the lump-sum option, changes in survivor benefits), you may need to check a variety of formulas to use in estimating your annuity.

There are many factors that could cause your preliminary estimate to go up or down. These include your age at the time of retirement; the type of retirement for which you apply; whether or not you elect survivor benefits; whether you elect an alternative annuity and lump-sum payment and whether you are receiving a military retirement or disability pension.

The final figure will be computed by the Office of Personnel Management. The preliminary figure will be the result of meetings between you and your retirement advisor in the personnel office of your agency.

FIGURING ANNUITIES

CSRS Formula. To compute your annuity under CSRS:

- 1.5% x high 3 average salary x 1st five years of service that applies to CSRS Component
- + 1.75% x high 3 average salary x amount of service that applies to the CSRS Component in excess of 5 years but not more than 10 years
- + 2.0% x high 3 average salary x amount of service that applies to the CSRS Component in excess of 10 years

The total of the three steps will give you your annuity.

For example:

Age 60

30 years of service that applies to the CSRS Component

$30,000 average salary

1.5% x $30,000 x 5	=	$ 2,250
1.75% x $30,000 x 5	=	$ 2,625
2.0% x $30,000 x 20	=	$12,000
		$16,875

FERS Non-Disability Annuity Computations

FERS Formula for Basic Annuity (without a CSRS Component)

- If retiree is under age 62 or has less than 20 years creditable service:

    1% x high 3 average salary x length of service

- If retiree is at least age 62 and has performed at least 20 years of creditable service:

    1.1% x high 3 average salary x length of service

Examples

- Age 60
    25 years of total service
    $40,000 average salary
    1.0% x $40,000 x 25   = $10,000

- Age 62
    25 years of total service
    $40,000 average salary
    1.1% x $40,000 x 25   = $11,000

FERS Combined Basic Annuity

- Sum of the Basic Annuity CSRS Component and the Basic Annual FERS Component

Example

    Age 60
    25 years applied to CSRS Component
    5 years applied to FERS Component
    $30,000 average salary

- Compute Basic Annual CSRS Component
    1.5% x $30,000 x 5   = $2,250
    1.75% x $30,000 x 5   = $2,625
    2.0% x $30,000 x 15   = $9,000
    CSRS Component $13,875

- Compute Basic Annual FERS Component
    1.0% x $30,000 x 5   = $1,500

- FERS Combined Basic Annuity
    $13,875 + $1,500   = $15,375

There are special provisions for computing the annuity of firefighters and law enforcement officers. Under the CSRS component they are entitled to 2.5 percent times their average "high-3" salary times the number of years served in a law enforcement or fire fighter position (not more than 20 years). To this they add 2 percent times their average "high-3" salary that applies to the CSRS component for years served in excess of 20 or that was not in law enforcement or fire fighting services. (Special rules apply to air traffic controllers.)

Under the FERS component they would take 1.7 percent times the average "high-3" salary times length of service that applies to the FERS component but not more than 20 years. To this figure they add 1 percent times the average "high-3" salary times years of service that usually applies to the FERS component in excess of 20 years. (If there is a CSRS component, the law enforcement/ fire fighter service taking place before the transfer to FERS does not count against the 20-year limitation for the special FERS computation.)

ANNUITY LIMITS

The basic annuity for any type retirement cannot exceed 80 percent of your high three average salary except for credit for unused sick leave (only counted under CSRS). To qualify for the top amount under CSRS you would need to have 41 years 11 months of service. Should you work more than 41 years 11 months, excess deposits will be applied to any redeposits you may owe. If you don't owe any, the excess deposits will be returned to you in a lump-sum (This 80 percent limitation does not apply to subsequent COLAs.)

Under FERS there is no 80 percent cap, probably because you would have to work for over 70 years to reach 80 percent. However, an employee who was under CSRS for many years and switched to FERS when given the opportunity could get a combined CSRS/FERS annuity of over 80 percent.

DISABILITY RETIREMENTS

For federal and postal employees retired on disability, the annuity is computed either on the guaranteed minimum or projected service to age 60, whichever is greater.

Employees who retire because of a disability are guaranteed a minimum retirement benefit. The guarantee benefits employees who are under 60 years of age at retirement and have less than 22 years of creditable service. The guarantee is based on two formulas which give credit for more service than the annuitant actually has.

- 40 percent computation. Annuity is computed as though the employee had served 21 years and 11 months; or,

- projected service through age 60. Annuity is computed as though the employee had worked to age 60 by adding projected service to actual service.

For example, an employee who retires involuntarily at age 40 with actual service of 10 years would have projected service of 20 years, giving him or her an annuity based on that service, or on 40 percent of actual salary, whichever is lower.

Guaranteed minimum computation will never exceed 40 percent. It may, however be less than that. Guaranteed minimums do not apply if you are receiving military retired pay or VA benefits in lieu of military retirement pay.

ANNUITY REDUCTIONS

Once the basic annuity has been computed under either FERS or CSRS it may be reduced for several reasons. These include:

- **Reduction for age.** This applies if the employee retires under early retirement or optional retirement based on a combination of age and length of service. The reduction for early optional or involuntary retirement applies only to the CSRS component. It equals ⅙ of 1 percent for each full month under age 55. The reduction will not be eliminated when the annuitant becomes 55.

Both the CSRS and the FERS component require a reduction for minimum retirement age (MRA) plus 10. The reduction equals 5/12 of 1 percent for each full month under age 62 at the time the annuity begins. The reduction will not be eliminated when the annuitant reaches 62. The FERS basic annuity will never be subject to reductions for either discontinued service/early optional retirement and minimum retirement age plus 10.

- **Reduction for Unpaid Deposit.** Applies only to the CSRS component. The reduction equals 10 percent of unpaid deposits for service prior to October 1982.

- **Reduction for Survivor Annuity.** The reduction for survivor annuity applies to the combined annual annuity, including the CSRS component if the annuity has one. Survivor benefit options are covered in Chapter 7. The reduction for a full survivor election is 10 percent of the basic annuity reduced for age and unpaid deposits. For partial survivor election the reduction is 5 percent of the basic annuity reduced for age and unpaid deposit. A court-ordered survivor annuity results in a deduction of 10 percent of the court ordered base.

- **Reduction for Alternative Annuity.** Under current law you have a choice as to how you would like to receive your annuity benefit. One option allows you to take a lump-sum payment equal to the amount of your contributions to the retirement system and a reduced monthly annuity. For further discussion of this option see Chapter 4.

SPECIAL RETIREMENT SUPPLEMENT

Some FERS employees may be eligible for a Special Retirement Supplement if they retire before age 62. Social Security benefits cannot start before age 62 under normal circumstances. The supplement approximates the portion of a full career Social Security benefit you would receive at age 62 that was earned while you were under FERS. The supplement ends at age 62 when Social Security benefits normally become available, even if you are not eligible for such benefits. Check with your personnel office for a detailed outline of the rules required to qualify for the special retirement supplement.

COST OF LIVING RAISES

All retirees receive an annual annuity increase based on a cost-of-living (COLA) formula approved by Congress. This is one of the most important provisions of federal retirement programs. Studies show that private sector pensions replace one-third or less of the loss to inflation of the purchasing power of retiree benefits. In contrast, CSRS, FERS, and Social Security return annuities to their full value each year (unless specifically modified by changes in law).

The number of people affected by the COLAs make this a costly program. Each 1 percent of inflation adjustments adds 12 percent to the long-term cost of the program.

The COLA increase for retirees and survivor annuitants is effective each December and payable in January checks. The amount is based on the difference between the third quarter Consumer Price Index for Urban Wage Earners and Clerical Workers (CPI-W) for one year and the same period during the previous year. The number of months for which the COLA is received is prorated over the number of months during the year the employee was retired. For example, a person retiring in May would receive 7/12 of the COLA and in October, 2/12 of the COLA.

Over the last decade increases ranged from a high of 8.7 percent in 1983 to a low of 0 in 1986. Raises in recent years have been:

> 1987—1.3 percent
>
> 1988—4.2 percent
>
> 1989—4.0 percent
>
> 1990—4.7 percent
>
> 1991—5.4 percent

Remember that CSRS retirees get the full amount of the COLA.

The amount of the FERS increase depends on the annual change in the CPI-W for the year. If the CPI-W rises 3 percent or more, the benefits are increased by the CPI-W minus one percentage point. If the CPI-W increases by 2 to 3 percent, the adjustment will be 2 percent. If the CPI-W increase is 2 percent or less, the adjustment will be equal to the CPI-W.

In any case, Congress has the final say on the size of the increase.

THE OUTGO

The amount of money you will have coming in is relatively easy to compute. You have cut and dried formulas that determine the amount of your annuity. Figuring how much money you are going to need is a more complicated process.

Many factors will affect the amount of money you will need to maintain a reasonable standard of living. These include such things as the size of your family. Do you still have children in school? Do you have aging parents who will need your financial as well as emotional support? Do you own your own home or do you rent? Is the car paid for? Are you free of debt or do you have a plastic ax hanging over your head each month as the charge card bills arrive?

Some financial events occurring shortly after your retirement may give you a distorted view of how much money you will have coming in.

Be aware that you will be receiving some "one time" large checks. These include pay for accrued annual leave, which comes to you shortly after retirement. You also will be receiving your last salary check since there is a lag between time worked and payroll periods. OPM will begin paying you an estimated annuity check for the first couple of months after you retire. This check will be smaller than your regular annuity checks. When the final figure is determined you will receive a "catch-up" check to make up for the difference between the estimated annuity and the actual amount due you. Added to this you may have a delayed award or other special payment which would come after you retire.

If you are one of the few who can and do take a lump-sum payment for your retirement contributions you will receive one or more sizeable checks shortly after retirement. While federal taxes will be deducted from the lump-sum payments, you still will be left with a large amount of cash. Since the lump-sum payment cannot be rolled over into an IRA account, any interest or dividends you earn when you invest the money will be taxable in the year in which it is received.

Adding to this sudden influx of money will be the fact that you probably will be paying less for your medical expenses and will no longer have retirement contributions deducted from your income. If you retire under FERS you also will see an end to Social Security deducted from your check.

The sudden receipt of all this money may give you a distorted picture of the amount you will have for expenses once the extra "goodies" have been exhausted. Avoid the temptation to go out and make major purchases or sudden moves as a result of what seems like a windfall. Some months down the pike you may wish you had been more cautious.

Get together with your spouse and figure out your projected expenses per month. Include figures for housing, food, transportation, clothing, recreation, medical expenses and miscellaneous general expenses. Add them all up and you have your expenses for the month.

Under housing include the cost of your house payment or rent if any. If you plan a major change in your housing arrangements, include the projected cost figure. You will continue to need to eat in retirement. It may cost you less, but don't count on it. My wife and I attended a retirement seminar in which the speaker said we could save money since we probably would "eat out less" once we are retired. My wife responded that we might have to reconsider our retirement plans if retiring meant a drastic cut in our living standards.

There will, of course, be some changes in your spending habits. There also will be alternate ways in which you can still maintain a reasonable standard of living without busting the budget. These will be discussed in detail in the chapter on changing life styles.

Clothing cost is an item that must be included in your list of expenses. Those suits or dresses you wore during your working years will wear out. They may go out of style or you may retire to an area which will require a wardrobe different than what you have accumulated.

When you budget for transportation be sure to include travel expenses. A plan to travel and visit the kids may be exciting. It also can be expensive. If you use the family car it will require maintenance and upkeep in addition to the cost of fuel, insurance and an occasional car wash.

Medical expenses are an important consideration in your budget. You probably will carry over your health benefits. While part of these will be subsidized by the government, you still will have a premium to pay.

Even if you are covered by Medicare and switch to a lower cost plan during the annual "open season," it could still cost $800 or more a year. You also will have to budget for any other insurance coverage you want to keep.

Also included may be money needed to pay alimony or child support or any other expenses for which you may be liable. Nursing home care for elderly parents could prove a major drain on your resources unless you have budgeted for them.

Since annuity checks come once a month you probably will be paying bills on that schedule and will want to budget accordingly. Fill in the blanks with what you think your expenses are likely to be:

Housing	$ _____
Food	$ _____
Clothing	$ _____
Insurance	$ _____
Travel & Recreation	$ _____
Miscellaneous Expenses	$ _____
Emergency Funds	$ _____
Total Monthly Expenses	$ _____

Now is the time to compare the amount that you will have coming in and the amount you will need to meet your monthly expenditures. The amount of a "shortfall" between what you have and what you need should be a key factor in determining if you are financially ready to retire at this time.

If the amount you need will require spending every cent you get; or, if you have a margin of less than several hundred dollars between what you need and what you get, you should seriously consider working a few months or years longer. Remember that once you retire you are stuck with the decision. It probably won't be easy to get another job should you decide to return to work. You could end up needing to take a part-time job which would be less rewarding emotionally and financially than the job you are contemplating leaving. If that is true in your case, keep on working. You don't need the aggravation of money problems as you get ready to enjoy your retirement years.

It is hoped that you will have some additional sources of income in addition to your annuity check. You could have a sizeable investment income to augment your annuity if you made the most of your thrift savings investments as well as other types of investments.

An ideal goal would be to able to meet your living costs without having to eat into the principal of your savings. When added to your annuity, your investment income (interest, dividends, etc.) should help you to meet this goal.

There are many ways to augment your income and these will be discussed in detail in a later chapter.

One final financial note. Plan your investments in such a way as to leave some money quickly available for unexpected expenses. This generally would be equal to at least one month of your projected expenses.

It is a good idea to seek advice from your accountant, if you have one, or from an attorney skilled in investment matters. At the agency retirement seminars you will receive some guidance on budgeting but little or none on how to invest your savings. Don't make precipitous moves. You don't want to tie up all of your money in long-term instruments such as certificates of deposit. If you do so and then decide to buy a house, take a long vacation, or are faced with the emergency need for cash, you might have to pay a penalty to withdraw your money.

STATE TAXES

State governments have their hands out to reap some taxes from their residents who have retired. A rundown of the states that have no personal income tax and those that regard a portion of civil service annuities to be taxable will be found at the end of this chapter. Four states, California, Oregon, Massachusetts and New York require you to pay taxes on annuities earned while a resident of the state even though you no longer live there, although enforcement has been spotty. This is eventually going to have to be resolved in the courts.

Other things to watch the news for include:

- a case before a federal appeals court seeking to overturn the taxation of the lump-sum payments;

- proposed legislation in Congress to allow rollover of the payments into an Individual Retirement Account, and

- another legislative proposal, to exempt employees who must retire before age 55, such as law enforcement officers, air traffic controllers from the 10 percent penalty applied to those taking lump-sums before that age.

TAX EXEMPTIONS FOR CIVIL SERVICE ANNUITIES

States with No Personal Income Tax: Alaska, Connecticut, Florida, Nevada, New Hampshire, South Dakota, Tennessee, Texas, Washington, Wyoming.

States Exempting Total Amount of the Taxable Portion of Civil Service Annuities: Alabama, Hawaii, Illinois, Kansas, Massachusetts, New Mexico (beginning in 1989), New York (beginning in 1989), Pennsylvania.

States Allowing Partial Exemptions of the Taxable Portion of Civil Service and Other Annuities:

Arizona – $2,500 exclusion for all public pensions and military pensions.

Arkansas – $6,000.

Colorado –$20,000 for all pensioners 55+.

Delaware – Maximum exemption of $3,000 for those 60+. The exclusion for those under the age of 60 is $2,000 per year.

Georgia – $10,000 exclusion for those 62+ or disabled, of which $4,000 of the exclusion may be used to offset earned income on retirement income (interest, dividends, pensions).

Idaho – Exempt to $17,544 for married joint returns, or $11,700 for single. Must be 65+, or 62 and disabled. Amounts reduced by SS and/or RR benefits received.

Indiana – $2,000 for those 62+ reduced by any SS or RR benefits.

Iowa – $2,500, single; $5,000, joint return, at 55+, or disabled.

Kentucky – Federal civil service annuities excluded from gross income for persons 50+ subject to these limitations of earned income and maximum annuity exclusion:

$3,000 or less	–	$4,000 Excluded
$3,001 to $4,000	–	$3,000 Excluded
$4,001 to $5,000	–	$2,000 Excluded
$5,001 to $6,000	–	$1,000 Excluded
Over $6,000	–	None

Louisiana – $6,000, less the portion of federal income tax applicable to total exempt income per state formula. Must be 65+.

Maryland – Exempt to the maximum of $10,100, reduced by any SS or RR benefits received. Must be 65+ or totally and permanently disabled.

Michigan – $7,500, single; $10,000, joint return.

Minnesota – Eliminated exemption in 1988.

Mississippi – $5,000.

Missouri – $6,000 pension exclusion for pension income up to $25,000 for single and $32,000 for married couples. Above these income limits, there is no exclusion. Lump-sum distributions not otherwise included in Missouri: AGI, but subject to federal income tax under the IRC, Sec. 402, are taxed at 10% of the taxpayer's federal income tax liability.

Montana – $3,600.

New Jersey – $10,000, joint return; $7,500, single return; $5,000, married filing separately who receive no income in excess of $3,000 from remuneration or net profits from business. Must be 62+ or disabled.

North Carolina – $4,000 maximum.

North Dakota – $5,000. Amount reduced by SS benefits received.

Ohio – A credit from $25 to $200 for retirement income of $500 to $8,000.

Oklahoma – $5,500 for all public pensions.

Oregon – Exclusion up to $5,000 for retirees aged 62+, phased out above $30,000.

South Carolina – $3,000 for all public pensions.

Utah – $4,800 under 65; $7,500 if 65+. For joint return, for every $1 over $32,000, reduce by 50¢.

Virginia – Any retiree aged 55+ whose total retirement income is $16,000 or less may exclude up to $16,000. If total retirement income exceeds $40,000, it is fully taxable. For amounts between $16,000 and $40,000 the amount excluded is phased in so that for taxable years 1991 and after, the subtraction amount of $16,000 is reduced by $1 for every $3 of retirement income greater than $16,000. For 1990, 75% of the amount is excludable.

West Virginia – $2,000 pension exclusion for federal pensions.

Wisconsin – Exempted federal retirees who were employed prior to December 31, 1963.

States Taxing the Taxable
Portion of Civil Service Annuities

California, District of Columbia, Maine, Missouri, Nebraska, Rhode Island, Vermont.

District of Columbia — Those persons 62+ on or before December 31, 1986, may exclude $3,000 from the gross amount of their pension or annuity that was subject to District of Columbia income tax.

States Not Listed Have No Special Tax Provisions Affecting Civil Service Annuities.

Also, States Have Varying Exemptions from Income for Persons 62+ or 65+ and Minimum Income Levels Subject to Tax Which Have Not Been Listed Here.

Abbreviations:

SS = Social Security; RR = Railroad Retirement; AGI = Adjusted Gross Income

NOTE: For 55+, 62+, 65+, read age 55 and over, age 62 and over, age 65 and over, etc.

NOTE: A certain number of states now have withholding agreements with the federal government whereby its residents commuting to and working in another state may request a voluntary payroll deduction to apply to state-of-residence income tax obligation.

NOTE: In addition to the state taxes, many cities have their own income tax regulations. Check with your local municipal offices for current regulations.

CHAPTER 4
INSURANCE

For most federal employees life and health insurance coverage has been virtually automatic. Once you selected the coverage you wanted the premiums were deducted from your check. No further thought was given to insurance until the open season each year when there was an opportunity to change coverage or carrier.

Now, as you prepare to enter your golden years, it is important to reflect on your life and health insurance needs. While you will want to keep adequate coverage, there is no sense in making yourself "insurance poor" through excessive coverage at a time when you will have less income.

HEALTH INSURANCE

Eligibility to continue coverage applies equally to CSRS and FERS retirees. If you are now covered under the Federal Employees Health Benefit Program (FEHB) you probably will want to continue it in retirement. **Should you discontinue coverage after retirement, you will not be permitted to re-enroll.**

You are eligible to continue your health insurance coverage into retirement if you:

- retire on an immediate annuity.

- are covered by the FEHB Program on the date of retirement.

- have been continuously covered for the five years immediately preceding retirement or, since your first opportunity to enroll.

- have been covered under a family member's enrollment or have been covered by CHAMPUS.

    However, for CHAMPUS to count, you must be enrolled in FEHB on retirement and have been continuously covered under FEHB/CHAMPUS for five years or from the date on which you were first eligible for the coverage. (if less than five years).

If your annuity is too small to cover the insurance premiums, you can make your payments directly to OPM. In such a situation coverage will be lost if premiums are not sent to OPM. Once you have elected to send in premiums you can never have them deducted from your checks, even if your annuity increases enough to make that possible.

In most cases the benefits for which you qualified as an employee will continue into retirement. Under certain plans dental care, eye examinations, hearing tests, physical examinations and other special programs will end when you retire.

The health insurance premiums you pay will be the same except that you will pay once a month instead of twice. The premium automatically will be deducted from your monthly annuity check.

"In most cases the benefits for which you qualified as an employee will continue into retirement."

Continuing your government health insurance does not mean you will never have an opportunity to change the coverage. (You can make changes during the open seasons). In addition, changes in your family situation may mean you no longer need coverage for your spouse or dependents. In such cases you can switch from "self and family" to "self only" at any time.

Changing from "self only" to "self and family" coverage is a bit more limited. It is only allowed if:

- there is a change in your marital status. This could be the result of marriage or remarriage. It could also occur with the birth or adoption of a child.

In the event of a divorce or separation you might want to switch from "self and family" to "self." Such a change could be made only during the open season.

You can only change the type coverage you have (for instance, going from high option to low option) under the following conditions:

- when there is a change in your marital status such as divorce, remarriage or death of a spouse.

- when you become eligible for Medicare (at age 65). Then you may find it less expensive to switch from the high option to low option coverage. Eligible retirees who are enrolled in a high option plan might consider changing to low option after the spouse becomes eligible for Medicare. Once you reach 65 Medicare becomes the prime insurer and your other health benefit plans offer supplemental benefits. It may be to your advantage to switch to a lower option coverage at this time.

- during any open season.

LIFE INSURANCE

There are rules for continuing your life insurance after you retire in the same way there are rules governing continuing your health benefits.

At retirement you will have to to choose from a number of options for continuing your life insurance coverage. Here is a look at each of the options:

Basic Coverage. Basic coverage is based on your annual base pay rounded to the next $1,000, plus $2,000. The only difference in this coverage after you retire is the loss of the accidental death and dismemberment coverage.

You can go one of three ways in deciding how to continue your basic coverage:

- you can continue the policy with no reduction in the coverage. To do this (if you retire on or after January 1, 1990) you will have to pay a monthly premium of $.401 per $1,000 of basic coverage. You also will have to pay an additional premium of $1.69 per thousand of coverage until you reach age 65. At age 65 the $.401 premium ends but the $1.69 continues.

- you can accept a 50 percent reduction in coverage (with the reduction beginning at age 65). At that point it reduces 1 percent per month until the coverage reaches 50 percent. If you elect this option you pay $.401 per $1,000 of basic coverage plus $.52 per $1,000 of coverage until age 65. The $.401 ends at age 65 but the additional premium continues.

- you can elect a 75 percent reduction in coverage, with the reduction beginning at age 65. The coverage reduces 2 percent per month until the 25 percent level is reached. If you elect this option and, if you retired before January 1, 1990, the coverage continues without cost. Employees separating after that date will pay the same monthly premium as regular employees ($.401 per $1,000 of basic coverage) until reaching age 65.

Option A. This is the standard option providing $10,000 coverage for all employees. The cost of the coverage is based on the age of the retiree. The monthly cost ranges from 87 cents per month per $1,000 of coverage for employees under 35 to $15.17 per month for employees between 60 and 64. The coverage is free for those 65 and over who retired before January 1, 1990, and those retired on workers' compensation.

Option B. This option gives you the chance to buy additional life insurance. Coverage may be increased in multiples of 1, 2, 3, 4, or 5 times annual basic pay. The coverage is rounded to the next $1,000. The smallest number of multiples in force during the five years of service immediately preceding retirement is carried into retirement. The cost is based on the age of the retiree and ranges from $0.08 per $1,000 pr month for those under 35 to $1.70 per $1,000 per month for those age 60 and over. Coverage is free after the end of the calendar month in which a retiree or a person collecting workers' compensation turns 65.

Option C. Family. This option provides $5,000 worth of insurance for the spouse and $2,500 for each eligible child. The cost is determined by the age of the retiree, not by the number of family members. The cost ranges from $0.65 per $1,000 of coverage for those under 35, to $6.06 per month per $1,000 for those age 60 and over. There is no charge for a retiree or workers' compensation recipient after the end of the calendar month in which he or she becomes 65.

Employees can carry Options A, B and C, into retirement if

they are eligible to continue basic coverage, have been covered for the last five years of employment or since the first opportunity to enroll. Options B and C reduce 2 percent per month for 50 months until the insurance terminates.

Regardless of which option you choose, you will have to designate a beneficiary. OPM has established an order of preference under which benefits will be paid. The beneficiary you designate has first right to your estate. He or she is followed by the widow or widower; children and/or dependents of any deceased children; parents; the executor or administrator of the estate; and the next of kin of the beneficiaries if those you designated die before you.

There are many factors to consider as you weigh the options to continue life insurance and health insurance. For most people retiring in the next few years the reduction of life insurance probably is a good choice. Unless you have a very large estate, you probably need only minimum insurance to cover your burial costs. Take the money you save in premiums and use it to take an extra vacation. You'll probably live longer.

The picture will change as the number of employees covered by the Federal Employees Retirement System (FERS) increases. The plan, at least as now presented, could find retirees in the next couple of decades retiring with a nest egg of up to a million dollars. The amount, of course, will depend on whether the employee has made substantial contributions to his or her Thrift Savings Plan account and the performance of the plans in which the funds are invested, as well.

Leaving such a large estate could subject your heirs to heavy inheritance taxes. If you want to avoid creating such a problem, talk to your financial advisor. There are many mechanisms—including living trusts—that will help shelter the money from taxation. You can also carry sufficient life insurance to cover the taxes.

If you carry your health benefits into retirement you should keep a sharp eye on the coverage you need. Changes would be appropriate if you get married; divorced; lose a spouse through death; remarry; or your dependents reach an age when they are no longer eligible for coverage.

LIFE INSURANCE—COVERAGE AND COSTS

Basic—Annual basic pay (rounded to next $1,000) plus $2,000

Cost for retirees: free for persons retiring before January 1, 1990, 40.1 cents per $1,000 for those retiring on or after January 1, 1990, who are under age 65 at retirement; this premium is in addition to the premiums required if you elect either the 50% or No Reduction schedule.

Optional A – Standard

$10,000 coverage
Cost is determined by age of retiree (see table)

	Monthly Rate
Under 35	0.87
35–39	1.08
40–44	1.73
45–49	2.82
50–54	4.77
55–59	9.75
60–64	15.17
65 and over	FREE if retired or on Worker's Comp.

Option B – Additional

Available in multiples of 1, 2, 3, 4, or 5 times annual basic pay (rounded to next higher $1,000 before multiplying)

Cost determined by age of retiree (see table)

	Monthly Rate
Under 35	.087 per $1,000
35–39	.108
40–44	.173
45–49	.282
50–54	.477
55–59	.975
60–64	1.842
65 and over	FREE if retired or on Worker's Comp.

Option C – Family

$5,000 for spouse; $2,500 for each eligible child

Cost determined by age of retiree—not by number of family members. (see table)

	Monthly Rate
Under 35	.65
35–39	.67
40–44	1.13
45–49	1.52
50–54	2.38
55–59	3.79
60–64	6.07
65 and over	FREE if retired or on Worker's Comp.

LIFE INSURANCE AFTER RETIREMENT

Types of Insurance	What happens after retirement?	What happens after age 65?	Can this option be changed after retirement?
Basic Life (Regular)	Premium depends on reduction elected at retirement	Reduction depends on election made at time of retirement	Can be cancelled
Basic Life Reduction **(1) 75%**—free if retired before 1–1–90; 40.1 cents per $1,000 coverage for those retiring on or after 1–1–90 who are under age 65 at retirement. **(2) 50%**—40.1 cents per $1,000 coverage (if retired on or after 1–1–90 and under age 65), PLUS 52 cents per $1,000 coverage. **(3) no reduction**— 40.1 cents per $1,000	Employee chooses at retirement; begins paying premiums **at** retirement	Premium ends if annuitant chose (1); Annuitant continues to pay the **extra** (but not the 40.1 cents per $1,000) premiums if he/she chose (2) or (3); reduction begins	Can change to 75% reduction, or cancelled

coverage (if retired on or after 1-1-90 and under age 65), PLUS $1.69 per $1,000 coverage.			Can be cancelled
Option A - Standard $10,000	Must pay premiums until age 65	Free, but coverage reduces 2% per month down to **25%**	
Option B - Additional (1, 2, 3, 4, or 5 times annual salary)	Must pay premium until age 65; can carry into retirement the **lowest** number of multiples elected during the last 5 years of employment	Free, but coverage reduces 2% per month down to **nothing**	Can cancel or change to fewer multiples
Option C - Family $5,000 for spouse $2,500 for each eligible child	Must pay premium until age 65; one premium covers the family	Free, but coverage reduces 2% per month down to **nothing**	Can be cancelled

Source: Office of Personnel Management

HEALTH INSURANCE CHECK LIST

Your insurance decisions will be made easier if you have some basic information with you when you meet with your retirement counselor. This checklist will help you gather the information you will need.

1. What Federal Employee Health Benefits (FEHB) coverage do you now hold?

   Plan Name _____

   Enrollment Type (self only or self and family) _____

   Option (high or low) _____

2. Will you be eligible to continue your health benefits when your retire? (Check eligibility rules in this chapter).

3. Are you currently covered as a family member on your spouse's health benefit plan? If so, have you compared the cost and benefits of each plan to see which is best for you?

4. Do you presently have any other health benefit plan? Have you compared the benefits under the different plans? You may find it possible to save money by dropping one of the plans or reducing one to a lower option, thereby cutting cost.

5. Are your family members now covered by your health benefit plan? Will they continue to be covered after you retire? If they are adequately protected by other insurance, you can cut cost by reducing your coverage from "family" to "self only."

6. How much are you now paying for health insurance per month? $_____ . Remember that the deduction on your pay stub is based on two payments a month. The premium you pay in retirement will only be collected once a month. To determine what the cost will be see rates in this chapter.

7. If you are still working, are you familiar with the coverage provided by your current plan? Review that coverage. You may find it advantageous to switch carriers during the open season if their benefits are better than what you now have.

8. Are you or your spouse eligible for Medicare at this time? Medicare becomes the primary carrier once you reach age 65. You may find it advisable to switch to a low option policy once Medicare is paying the larger part of your medical bills.

LIFE INSURANCE CHECK LIST

After you decide what health benefits you will carry into retirement you should take a close look at your life insurance coverage. Here are some questions that will help you decide how much and what type insurance you need.

1. What Federal Employee Government Life Insurance (FEGLI) do you now hold?

    ❏ Basic Amount $ _____

    ❏ Option A: Standard $ 10,000

    ❏ Option B: (Additional coverage)   Amount $ _____

    ❏ Option C: (Family coverage) $5,000 for spouse; 2,500 for each child $ _____

2. How much of your coverage will you be able to carry into retirement?

    Basic $ _____

    Option A $ _____

    Option B $ _____

    Option C $ _____

3. What post-retirement reduction of basic life insurance have you chosen?

    ❏ 75 percent reduction.

    ❏ 50 percent reduction.

    ❏ No reduction.

Review costs of each option outlined earlier in this chapter.

Now that you have assembled all of those figures you can determine what your monthly premium will be after you retire.

     Basic Life Reduction $ _____

     Option A Standard $ _____

     Option B Additional $ _____

     Option C Family $ _____

Add to this figure the premiums on any other life insurance policies you own $ _____

By using this checklist you can quickly determine if your life insurance coverage is too high, too low, or just about right. If it is higher than necessary you can cancel some coverage and cut costs. If it is too low you might want to check out the cost of supplemental coverage. If it is "just right," congratulations on being an astute planner.

A bit of advice before leaving the subject of life insurance coverage. Check with your personnel office to verify that your Official Personnel File accurately reflects your wishes as far as insurance coverage and the disposition of your estate. Be sure you have designated a valid beneficiary and that your choice is recorded in your file. If you have any questions about the order of precedence in which beneficiaries may be named, review the data provided in this chapter.

CHAPTER 5
SOCIAL SECURITY

Many federal government and postal employees will have spent some time in jobs covered by the Social Security System. If you are one of them, you may be entitled to some benefits because of this covered employment. If so, you can include them in your figuring as you calculate your retirement budget.

Social Security is a package of protection covering retirement, survivors and disability insurance. It protects you and your family while you work and after you retire. FERS employees are automatically covered by Social Security; CSRS employees can qualify by working in the private sector.

It is important to know that Social Security never was intended to replace all of your earnings once you retired. If you qualify for benefits you will have an important supplement to your government pension.

Social Security numbers are impressive. About 27.5 million people receive monthly Social Security retirement cash benefits. This total includes about 24 million retired workers and 3.5 million of their eligible family members and survivors.

To qualify to receive benefits you must first have credit for a certain amount of work in jobs covered by the Social Security system. You can earn a maximum of four credits per year. These credits may have been earned at any time since the Social Security system was created in 1936.

All eligible employees and self-employed people earn Social Security credits the same way. In 1990 you receive one credit for each $520 of annual earnings up to a maximum of four based on annual earnings of $2,080 or more. The amount needed to earn a credit will increase automatically in future years as average wages increase.

If you work for a while and then leave the covered occupation the credits you have earned will be kept on your Social Security (SSA) records. You can add to them later if you return to work in a covered occupation.

If you are fully insured when you reach retirement age, you and certain members of your family can receive monthly benefits.

You can start receiving Social Security retirement benefits at age 62. Monthly Social Security benefits also are paid to eligible spouses and children of workers who have retired.

A divorced spouse who has been divorced at least two years can receive benefits at 62 whether or not his or her former spouse receives them. Their marriage must have lasted ten years or more. The former spouse must be at least 62 and eligible for Social Security benefits, regardless of whether he or she has retired.

Federal and postal employees are required to pay a portion of their salaries to cover the cost of Medicare. At age 65 they will become eligible to collect on the benefits such insurance provides.

There are two parts to Medicare, hospital insurance and medical insurance. Medicare is handled by the Health Care Financing Administration, not by Social Security. But, the people at Social Security offices will help you apply for Medicare and answer your questions about the program. In our research we have found the Social Security workers to be both cooperative and knowledgeable. They have a toll-free number (1-800-2345-SSA) and will answer calls between 9 a.m. and 4:30 p.m. (EST) Monday through Friday.

The hospital insurance part of Medicare helps pay the cost of inpatient hospital care and certain kinds of follow-up care. The medical insurance part helps pay the cost of physicians' services and certain other medical items including services not covered by hospital insurance. About three fourths of the cost of the medical insurance is paid from the general revenues of the federal government. Enrollees pay a basic premium ($28.60 a month through 1990). This premium rises each year.

The Social Security Administration recommends that you apply for Medicare about three months before you become eligible for benefits even if you do not plan to retire. When you apply for hospital insurance you will be automatically enrolled for the medical insurance portion of the coverage. When your Medicare coverage begins it will become your primary health insurance carrier. This means that all claims will be processed first by Medicare and then referred to your supplemental carrier if Medicare does not cover the full amount.

Application is necessary before you can receive any SSA benefits. If you plan to retire before you reach age 65 (and are eligible for SSA) it is important to apply for monthly benefits no later than the last day of the month you want benefits to begin.

When you apply for benefits you will have to furnish certain documents. They include:

- your Social Security card or a record of the number,

- your birth certificate (other proofs of age may be substituted if your birth was not recorded),

- children's birth certificates and Social Security numbers if they are applying for benefits,

- evidence showing your recent earnings (last year's W-2 forms or a copy of last year's self-employment tax return),

- proof of the worker's death if you are applying for survivor's benefits.

Do not delay applying even if you lack one or more of the documents required. The people at Social Security can tell you of other documents that can be substituted.

If you are eligible for Social Security and you elect to work after retirement you are limited in the amount you can earn and still collect benefits. The annual exempt amount for 1991 is $9,720 for people 65 through 69 and $7,080 for persons under 65. There is no limit for those 70 and older.

If your earnings go over the annual exempt amount, SSA will withhold $1 in benefits for each $2 of earnings above the limit for people under 65. For people 65 through 69, $1 in benefits will be withheld for every $3 over the limit.

A special rule allows people who retire during the year to receive benefits for the remainder of the year regardless of total annual earnings. Under this rule you can receive a full benefit for any month of entitlement in which your wages do not exceed the monthly exempt amount and you do not perform substantial services in self-employment. The monthly exempt amount in 1991 was $810 if you were 65 through 69 and $590 if you were under 65. It is important to note that only your earnings from employment or self-employment count. Income from savings, investments, pensions or insurance does not count.

If you return to work after you start receiving retirement benefits, your added earnings may result in higher benefits. Social Security will automatically refigure your benefit after the additional earnings are credited to your record.

Up to one-half of your benefits may be subject to federal income tax each year in which your adjusted gross income for federal tax purposes plus nontaxable interest income and one-half of your Social Security benefits exceed a base amount. The base amount is $25,000 for an individual and $32,000 for a couple filing jointly. The amount of the benefits subject to tax will be the smaller of one-half the benefits, or one-half the amount of combined income (adjusted gross income plus nontaxable interest plus one half of total benefits) in excess of the base amount.

At the end of each year you will receive a Social Security Benefit Statement (Form SSA-1099) in the mail. It will show the amount of benefits you received. The statement will be used in completing your federal income tax return if any of your benefits are subject to tax.

If you have taxable income, some Internal Revenue Service publications may be of help, especially Publication 554, *Tax Benefits for Older Americans*, and Publication 915, *Tax Information on Social Security Benefits*. These and other publications are available at local IRS offices.

Two of the most misunderstood provisions of the retirement system are the "Public Pension Offset" and the "Windfall Elimination Provision."

Under the *Public Pension Offset* the Social Security benefits a person receives as a spouse or surviving spouse will be reduced if that person also receives a pension based on government service which was not covered by Social Security.

Federal and postal employees who remain under CSRS are

subject to the reduction or offset. Under current law those who transferred to FERS are not because Social Security coverage is a part of FERS.

Here's how the offset works. If you retire from federal or postal service and also are eligible for Social Security benefits as a spouse or survivor, your Social Security benefit will be reduced. It is reduced because you are receiving a pension from the federal government based on earnings not covered by Social Security. For every $3 you receive from your CSRS pension, your Social Security spousal benefit is reduced by $2.

Example: Let's assume you were eligible for a $500 Social Security spousal benefit. Suppose you were also receiving a CSRS benefit amounting to $900 a month. The Public Pension Offset would be two-thirds of your monthly CSRS benefit or $600. Since the offset amount is larger than your Social Security benefit, your Social Security benefit would be eliminated.

This factor probably will not be significant for anyone who earns his or her own Social Security benefit based in whole or in part on FERS service. This is because earned Social Security benefits are usually larger than spousal benefits and Social Security will not pay both at the same time.

The Windfall Elimination provision reduces Social Security benefits for those who have less than 30 years of substantial coverage under Social Security and have earned a retirement benefit working in a job not covered by Social Security.

The provision was designed to eliminate the "windfall" that could result if you got a pension based on your government service and also got a full Social Security benefit because you had a few years of covered employment.

If you are covered by this provision, your Social Security benefits will be figured using a reduced benefit formula.

Social Security generally provides a higher proportion of benefits to lower income employees than it does to those who are paid more. The reduction that results from the Windfall Elimination provision, however, tends to cancel out this effect, particularly for those who reach age 62 in 1990 or later.

SOCIAL SECURITY CHECK LIST

❑ Check your employment records to see if you qualify for both a government annuity and a Social Security check.

❑ If you do not have enough employment covered by Social Security to qualify for a Social Security pension, determine how many quarters you lack and what it would take to acquire them (part-time jobs, etc.).

❑ Gather necessary documentation to validate your age and work records (Social Security card, birth certificate, marriage licenses, divorce papers).

❑ Check with the Social Security specialist in your personnel office to determine when to apply for benefits.

❑ Learn the earning limits on Social Security recipients. Plan your retirement earnings to stay within the limits unless you are willing to risk losing some of your benefits.

❑ Review tax publications available from IRS. They explain special tax rules for retirees.

❑ Be sure you understand pension offset and windfall rules since they could result in reduced benefits.

CHAPTER 6
SURVIVOR BENEFITS

One of the major advantages of the federal retirement system is the opportunity it offers to provide for our loved ones after we die. This opportunity comes to government employees at comparatively low cost.

You and your spouse probably figure you will live forever. However, since no one does, your retirement planning should include a clear decision on what benefits you want for your survivors.

In general, the same conditions govern the annuities paid to survivors of retirees under the CSRS and FERS systems. However, because of the coordination of FERS with survivor benefits under Social Security, the actual benefits payable to survivors are different and based on the circumstances of the survivor.

Knowing how the benefits work and how much they cost will save you from the hucksters who will be trying to sell you all sorts of supplemental insurance coverage. There is little chance private insurers can afford to match the benefits your survivors get when you elect one of the government options.

Of course, survivor benefits do not come without a price. The type benefit you elect will determine the amount by which your annuity will be reduced during your lifetime.

Here's a quick look at what the options you elect will provide and how much they will cost you:

Annuity with Survivor Benefit to Widow, Widower or Former Spouse. If you are married and elect a survivor annuity when you retire, your widow or widower will receive a monthly check after you die. If you don't want your spouse to receive an annuity, you have to request this option in writing. The waiver request must be signed by both you and your spouse. The only action that could block payment after that would be a court order obtained by a former spouse to protest the payment.

Electing this option will cost you 2.5 percent of the first $3,600 used as a base for survivor annuity; plus 10 percent of any amount over $3,600 used as a base for survivor annuity.

The amount of benefit under this option is either 50 percent or 25 percent of the retiree's total annuity, under FERS, and 55 percent under CSRS. You must have the consent of your spouse if you elect a survivor benefit of less than 50 percent under FERS or 55 percent under CSRS.

"You can help members of your family by keeping them informed of what they will have to do in the event of your death."

There may be times when you need to change to name of the spouse you listed as your beneficiary when you retire. It can happen if the spouse you named dies before you do, or if the marriage is otherwise dissolved. If you remarry after you retire, your new spouse can become eligible for your survivor benefits. Your written request for the change must be submitted no more than two years after your remarriage.

The law now provides that if your marriage is terminated by annulment, divorce or death of your spouse, your annuity will be recomputed.

If you are unmarried when you retire and later marry, you have two years in which to request a reduced annuity with survivor benefits to your spouse.

Once a change of election is accepted by OPM it cannot be changed again. A deposit covering the difference between the unreduced annuity and reduced annuity plus interest must be made if an employee marries or remarries after retirement.

To be eligible for a survivor benefit in the above circumstances, the spouse must be married to the retiree for at least nine months before his or her death or, if married less than nine months, be the parent of a child born of the marriage. A shorter time is acceptable if the death of the annuitant is the result of an accident.

Benefits to Former Spouses. A retiring employee can designate his or her former spouse as the beneficiary of survivor benefits. The benefit may be elected by the employee or ordered by a court decree. If the benefit is to be elected, the consent of the current spouse is required.

A court may order such a CSRS benefit in a divorce which took place before or after the 1985 law which established survivor benefits for former spouses. For FERS employees the divorce must have been on or after May 7, 1985. Such a court-ordered benefit has priority over the entitlement of the current spouse.

Benefits to eligible spouses and former spouses begin on the day after the death of the retiree or the first day of the second month after OPM receives a court order with the former spouse's claim to benefits.

Benefits for the current spouse end the last day of the month prior to the death of the retiree. Benefits also cease if the surviving spouse remarries before age 55. Benefits for former spouses end at the death of the retiree. They can be terminated earlier if the original court order is rescinded.

The survivor's annuity for a former spouse **cannot** be restored if the remarriage is terminated.

Survivor Benefits to Children. If, upon your death after retirement, you are survived by children, they could, regardless of the type of annuity you had elected, qualify for a survivor annuity.

To be eligible children must be unmarried and under the age of 18 or between ages 18 and 22 if a full-time student or disabled and incapable of self support. In any case, the retiree must have been contributing to the child's support at the time of the claim.

The total FERS benefit payable to all children will be reduced by the total amount of Social Security survivor benefits payable to all children.

Survivor Benefits to Person with Insurable Interest. There are situations in which you can designate as your beneficiary a person who has an insurable interest in your estate. For instance, you can designate a relative or friend as your beneficiary. There are complex rules governing such election and you would be wise to discuss them with your personnel office before attempting such selection.

At the end of this chapter you will find a table of annuity reductions for employees without spouses under either CSRS or FERS. You also will find a summary of rules governing the payment of death benefits.

Your executor should have a copy of your will and instructions on how to proceed to collect your benefits. If you don't have a will, make one out immediately. Avoid those bargain "will kits" that cost about $10 and give you a generic type will in which you just fill in the blanks. It is far wiser to spend a couple of hundred dollars and get your will prepared by a lawyer who knows the laws of your state and can assure you that your wishes can legally be carried out.

You can help members of your family by keeping them informed of what they will have to do in the event of your death. Tell them that Civil Service survivor benefits are not automatic— they require a formal application. Tell them your CSA number and provide them with a copy of this chapter. Keep this information together with your other valuable papers, insurance policies, house deeds, car titles etc. If you do all of these things you will be providing an invaluable service to your family.

FEDERAL ANNUITIES

To collect survivor benefits following the death of a retired federal worker the eligible survivor needs to follow a three-step procedure:

- Return any uncashed annuity checks to the return address shown on the Treasury Department's envelope in which the check was delivered. If annuity checks have been sent directly to a financial institution, promptly notify the institution of the annuitant's death. Ask that any payments received after the date of death be returned to the Treasury Department.
- Notify the Office of Personnel Management, Employee

Service and Records Center, Boyers, Pennsylvania 16017, of the death of the annuitant. Be sure to use the complete address including the ZIP Code. Its ZIP Code is unique to the Center and using this address will expedite the claim.

The letter of notification should include the full name of the deceased annuitant, the exact date of birth, the exact date of death, the CSA number of the deceased and the name, address and relationship of the person who is entitled to survivor benefits.

The Center will then send the survivor forms to be used in claiming benefits.

- Obtain a certified copy of the annuitant's death certificate to enclose when the benefit claim forms are filed. Wait until the claim forms arrive from OPM and send the certificate and the forms in the same package. Sending the information piecemeal will only delay the processing. While OPM is waiting for the application it will have completed certain preliminary actions to expedite the claim.

- It is essential the uncashed checks be returned to the Treasury. Government checks made payable to a deceased person cannot legally be cashed by anyone, even the executor or administrator of the estate. The Retirement Programs office cannot authorize a survivor benefit until the Treasury Department informs them that there are no outstanding checks payable to the deceased annuitant. However, any accrued annuity unpaid to the annuitant during his or her lifetime will be included in the benefit to the eligible survivor.

The Office of Retirement Programs also will provide the eligible survivor with an application for benefits under government life insurance programs. There is no need to contact any other office. In fact, the insurance companies cannot settle a claim until they get a certification of the deceased annuitant's insurance from OPM.

Once a certification is completed the survivor will be notified of any other benefits to which he or she may be entitled. These could include automatic health insurance coverage if the survivor has been covered by the annuitant's enrollment in any of the government's health benefit plans. To qualify, the survivor must be eligible for a survivor annuity beginning immediately after the death of the annuitant.

SOCIAL SECURITY

If you are insured by Social Security when you die, no matter what your age, your survivors may qualify for certain benefits.

Persons eligible to receive survivor benefits under Social Security include:

- Your surviving spouse at age 65 (or as early as age 60 if reduced benefits have been elected).

- Your surviving spouse, at any age, who is caring for your children who are under 16 or disabled.

- Your disabled surviving spouse at age 50 or older.

- Your unmarried children under 18 and those 18 or over who became disabled before age 22 and remain disabled.

- Your dependent parents age 62 or over.

- Your surviving divorced spouse (1) at age 60 or over (50 if disabled) who was married to you for 10 years or (2) at any age if caring for a child (under 16 or disabled) who is entitled to benefits under your record.

There are many technical rules limiting payments to survivors. If you are covered under Social Security, contact the Social Security Administration and ask for the latest summary of survivor benefits. The summary also can be obtained by calling the Social Security Administration at 1-800-2345-SSA. This is a toll-free call.

THRIFT PLAN DEPOSITS

If you die before satisfying the vesting requirements in your thrift savings deposits, all amounts in your account are automatically vested.

In general, when you die, the balance in your thrift account will be distributed to your designated beneficiary. If you did not designate a beneficiary, your account balance will be distributed according to the order of precedence prescribed by law: to your widow or widower; if none, to your child or children. If none, to your parents. If none, to your next of kin who is entitled to your estate under the laws of your state.

If you die after an insurance annuity has been purchased for you, benefits will be provided according to the annuity contract.

Death is not a pleasant thought. But, your survivors can be spared much unnecessary grief if you have planned carefully and kept all your records in order.

QUESTIONS AND ANSWERS ON SURVIVOR BENEFITS

Q. *When do I receive my annuity payment?*

A. You will be sent a statement telling you when to expect your first regular monthly payment. After that your annuity is paid on the first business day of each month.

Q. *How can I arrange to have my annuity payments deposited directly into my bank account?*

A. You need to go to your bank and ask for a Standard Form (SF) 1199A, Direct Deposit Sign-Up Form. When the form is completed the bank will mail the form to OPM and future checks will go into your bank account. You can have your checks sent to any bank, savings and loan association or federal or state chartered credit union.

Q. *Are there any advantages to having my annuity check payment deposited directly in a financial institution?*

A. Yes. It is a safeguard against your checks being stolen from your mailbox. It guarantees the bank will receive the payment and any possible delay will be avoided. It eliminates problems you may have in cashing your checks and allows your money to be available to you while you are away from home.

Q. *Can annuities be paid directly to children?*

A. Not usually. A child's annuity is paid to his or her legal guardian if one has been appointed. If there is no legal guardian, payment will be made to the person who has care and custody of the child.

Q. *What should be done with an annuity check that wasn't* *cashed before a survivor annuitant's death?*

To avoid any violation of the law, return any checks uncashed at the time of a survivor annuitant's death to the Director, Regional Financial Center, U.S. Treasury Department, P.O. Box 7367, Chicago, IL 60680 along with an explanation that the annuitant has died and the date of the death. If annuity payments are being deposited directly to the bank, your survivors should immediately notify the bank of your death.

Q. *Do I receive cost-of-living increases in my annuity payment?*

A. Yes. Survivor annuitants receive the cost-of-living increases provided by law.

Q. *Are my annuity payments subject to federal income tax?*

A. Yes, under rules administered by the Internal Revenue Service. If you have questions about the taxability of your annuity you should contact your local IRS office. The Civil Service Retirement System does not provide tax advice and does not distribute IRS publications. If your survivor annuity is taxable from the time it begins, federal income tax will be withheld from the check.

Q. *When does my survivor annuity begin and end?*

A. If you are a widow or widower your survivor annuity begins on whichever day is later; the day after the employee or retiree dies or the day after the entitlement of any former spouse ends if that entitlement prevents you from receiving a survivor annuity.

If you are a former spouse who is awarded a survivor annuity based on a qualifying court order, your survivor annuity begins on whichever day is later: the day after the employee or retiree dies or the day after the entitlement of any former spouse ends if that entitlement prevents you from receiving the survivor annuity.

Q. *Can I receive a civil service annuity and Social Security benefits at the same time?*

A. Yes. However, there may be a reduction in the amount of any Social Security benefit you receive based on your deceased spouse's service. This happens if you are entitled to receive a civil service annuity based on your own federal service. Contact any Social Security office for further details.

DEATH BENEFITS

1. *If Death Occurs Before Retirement.* If you leave no survivors who can qualify for a survivor annuity, your contributions to the Retirement Fund (but not your agency's contributions), with interest computed as explained in item Interest on Contributions, will be paid as a lump-sum death benefit.

If you leave survivors who qualify for a survivor annuity, no lump-sum death benefit is payable immediately. A lump-sum death benefit may be payable later if, when the survivors' annuities end, they have received in annuities an amount which is less than your contributions to the retirement fund, plus interest. The amount payable will be the difference between your contributions plus interest and the total paid out in survivor annuities.

2. *If Death Occurs After Retirement.* If you leave no survivors who can qualify for a survivor annuity, a lump-sum death benefit consisting of the annuity accrued to date of death is generally payable immediately. Also, if the total annuity paid to you is less than your contributions to the retirement fund, the difference will represent a balance payable as an immediate lump-sum death benefit.

If you leave survivors who qualify for a survivor annuity, no lump-sum death benefit (other than unpaid annuity accrued to date of death) is payable immediately. A lump-sum death benefit may be payable later if, when the survivors' annuities end, the total annuity paid to you and the survivors is less than your contributions to the retirement fund. The amount payable will be the difference between the total annuity paid and your contributions.

3. *To Whom Payable.* A lump-sum death benefit is payable to the person or persons shown below in the order indicated:

First: to the beneficiary designated by you;

Second: if you do not designate a beneficiary, to your widow or widower;

Third: if you leave no widow or widower, to your child or children in equal shares, with the share of any
(Continued on page 78)

CIVIL SERVICE RETIREMENT (CSRS) — COMPARATIVE ANNUAL ANNUITIES
Basic Annuity, and Reduced Annuity With Survivorship Benefits

| | PERCENT | | | | ANNUAL ANNUITY | | | | | | | |
| | | | | | Basic (No reductions) | | | | Basic with Survivorship Benefits (Reduction—2 1/2% on first $3,600, 10% on amounts above $3,600) | | | |
Average Annual Salary	Total First 5 Years	Total Second 5 Years	Total Percent First 10 Years	Each Add'l Year Over 10 Years	10 Years 16.25%	15 Years 26.25%	20 Years 36.25%	30 Years 56.25%	10 Years	15 Years	20 Years	30 Years
20,000	7.5%	8.75%	16.25%	2.0%	3,250	5,250	7,250	11,250	3,169	4,995	6,795	10,395
21,000	7.5%	8.75%	16.25%	2.0%	3,413	5,513	7,613	11,813	3,328	5,232	7,122	10,902
22,000	7.5%	8.75%	16.25%	2.0%	3,575	5,775	7,975	12,375	3,486	5,468	7,448	11,408
23,000	7.5%	8.75%	16.25%	2.0%	3,738	6,038	8,338	12,938	3,634	5,704	7,774	11,914
24,000	7.5%	8.75%	16.25%	2.0%	3,900	6,300	8,700	13,500	3,780	5,940	8,100	12,420
25,000	7.5%	8.75%	16.25%	2.0%	4,063	6,563	9,063	14,063	3,927	6,177	8,427	12,927
26,000	7.5%	8.75%	16.25%	2.0%	4,225	6,825	9,425	14,625	4,073	6,413	8,753	13,433
27,000	7.5%	8.75%	16.25%	2.0%	4,388	7,088	9,788	15,188	4,219	6,649	9,079	13,939
28,000	7.5%	8.75%	16.25%	2.0%	4,550	7,350	10,150	15,750	4,365	6,885	9,405	14,445
29,000	7.5%	8.75%	16.25%	2.0%	4,713	7,613	10,513	16,313	4,512	7,122	9,732	14,952
30,000	7.5%	8.75%	16.25%	2.0%	4,875	7,875	10,875	16,875	4,658	7,358	10,058	15,458
31,000	7.5%	8.75%	16.25%	2.0%	5,038	8,138	11,238	17,438	4,804	7,594	10,384	15,964
32,000	7.5%	8.75%	16.25%	2.0%	5,200	8,400	11,600	18,000	4,950	7,830	10,710	16,470
33,000	7.5%	8.75%	16.25%	2.0%	5,363	8,663	11,963	18,563	5,097	8,067	11,037	16,977
34,000	7.5%	8.75%	16.25%	2.0%	5,525	8,925	12,325	19,125	5,243	8,303	11,363	17,483
35,000	7.5%	8.75%	16.25%	2.0%	5,688	9,188	12,688	19,688	5,389	8,539	11,689	17,989
36,000	7.5%	8.75%	16.25%	2.0%	5,850	9,450	13,050	20,250	5,535	8,775	12,015	18,495
37,000	7.5%	8.75%	16.25%	2.0%	6,013	9,713	13,413	20,813	5,682	9,012	12,342	19,002
38,000	7.5%	8.75%	16.25%	2.0%	6,175	9,975	13,775	21,375	5,828	9,248	12,668	19,508
39,000	7.5%	8.75%	16.25%	2.0%	6,338	10,238	14,138	21,938	5,974	9,484	12,994	20,014

Income												
40,000	7.5%	8.75%	16.25%	2.0%	6,500	10,500	14,500	22,500	6,120	9,720	13,320	20,520
41,000	7.5%	8.75%	16.25%	2.0%	6,663	10,763	14,863	23,063	6,267	9,957	13,647	21,027
42,000	7.5%	8.75%	16.25%	2.0%	6,825	11,025	15,225	23,625	6,413	10,193	13,793	21,533
43,000	7.5%	8.75%	16.25%	2.0%	6,988	11,288	15,588	24,188	6,559	10,429	14,299	22,039
44,000	7.5%	8.75%	16.25%	2.0%	7,150	11,550	15,950	24,750	6,705	10,665	14,625	22,545
45,000	7.5%	8.75%	16.25%	2.0%	7,313	11,813	16,313	25,313	6,852	10,902	14,952	23,052
46,000	7.5%	8.75%	16.25%	2.0%	7,475	12,075	16,675	25,875	6,998	11,138	15,278	23,558
47,000	7.5%	8.75%	16.25%	2.0%	7,638	12,338	17,038	26,438	7,144	11,374	15,604	24,064
48,000	7.5%	8.75%	16.25%	2.0%	7,800	12,600	17,400	27,000	7,290	11,610	15,390	24,570
49,000	7.5%	8.75%	16.25%	2.0%	7,963	12,863	17,763	27,563	7,437	11,718	16,257	25,077
50,000	7.5%	8.75%	16.25%	2.0%	8,125	13,125	18,125	28,125	7,582	12,082	16,582	25,582
51,000	7.5%	8.75%	16.25%	2.0%	8,287	13,387	18,487	28,687	7,728	12,318	16,908	26,088
52,000	7.5%	8.75%	16.25%	2.0%	8,450	13,650	18,850	29,250	7,875	12,555	17,235	26,595
53,000	7.5%	8.75%	16.25%	2.0%	8,612	13,912	19,212	29,812	8,021	12,791	17,561	27,101
54,000	7.5%	8.75%	16.25%	2.0%	8,775	14,175	19,575	30,375	8,168	13,028	17,888	27,608
55,000	7.5%	8.75%	16.25%	2.0%	8,938	14,438	19,938	30,938	8,314	13,264	18,214	28,114
56,000	7.5%	8.75%	16.25%	2.0%	9,100	14,700	20,300	31,500	8,460	13,500	18,540	28,620
57,000	7.5%	8.75%	16.25%	2.0%	9,263	14,963	20,663	32,063	8,607	13,737	18,867	29,127
58,000	7.5%	8.75%	16.25%	2.0%	9,425	15,225	21,025	32,625	8,753	13,973	19,193	29,633
59,000	7.5%	8.75%	16.25%	2.0%	9,588	15,488	21,388	33,188	8,899	14,209	19,519	30,139
60,000	7.5%	8.75%	16.25%	2.0%	9,750	15,750	21,750	33,750	9,045	14,445	19,845	30,825
61,000	7.5%	8.75%	16.25%	2.0%	9,913	16,013	22,113	34,313	9,192	14,682	20,172	31,152
62,000	7.5%	8.75%	16.25%	2.0%	10,075	16,275	22,475	34,875	9,338	14,918	20,498	31,658
63,000	7.5%	8.75%	16.25%	2.0%	10,238	16,538	22,838	35,438	9,484	15,154	20,824	32,164
64,000	7.5%	8.75%	16.25%	2.0%	10,400	16,800	23,200	36,000	9,630	15,390	21,150	32,760
65,000	7.5%	8.75%	16.25%	2.0%	10,563	17,063	23,563	36,563	9,777	15,627	21,477	33,177
66,000	7.5%	8.75%	16.25%	2.0%	10,725	17,325	23,925	37,125	9,923	15,863	21,803	33,683
67,000	7.5%	8.75%	16.25%	2.0%	10,888	17,588	24,288	37,688	10,069	16,099	22,129	34,189
68,000	7.5%	8.75%	16.25%	2.0%	11,050	17,850	24,650	38,250	10,215	16,335	22,455	34,695
69,000	7.5%	8.75%	16.25%	2.0%	11,213	18,113	25,013	38,813	10,362	16,572	22,782	35,202

CIVIL SERVICE RETIREMENT TABLE FOR CSRS EMPLOYEES
Monthly Annuities Computed Under Basic Formulae
(Second line of each salary level reflects annuity with survivor deduction.)

Length of service cannot include any service for which a refund has been paid, unless the required redeposit is made before retirement is effective.

Basic annuity is subject to reduction if (a) deductions are not in the fund for any service since August 1, 1920, (b) retirement—except for disability—is before age 55, (c) a survivor-type annuity is elected at retirement.

Highest 3 Year Average Salary	YEARS OF CREDITABLE SERVICE																	Amounts For Each Add'l Yr. Unlisted*
	5	10	15	16	17	18	19	20	21	22	23	24	25	30	35	40	42	
20,000	125	271	438	471	504	538	571	604	638	671	704	738	771	938	1,104	1,271	1,333	33
	122	264	416	446	476	506	536	566	596	626	656	686	716	866	1,016	1,166	1,223	
22,000	138	298	481	518	555	591	628	665	701	738	775	811	848	1,031	1,215	1,398	1,467	36
	134	290	456	489	522	555	588	621	654	687	720	753	786	951	1,116	1,281	1,343	
24,000	150	325	525	565	605	645	685	725	765	805	845	885	925	1,125	1,325	1,525	1,600	40
	146	315	495	531	567	603	639	675	711	747	783	819	855	1,035	1,215	1,395	1,463	
26,000	163	352	569	612	655	699	742	785	829	872	915	959	1,002	1,219	1,435	1,652	1,733	43
	158	339	534	573	612	651	690	729	768	807	846	885	924	1,119	1,314	1,509	1,583	
28,000	175	379	613	659	706	753	799	846	893	939	986	1,033	1,079	1,313	1,546	1,779	1,867	46
	171	364	574	616	658	700	742	784	826	868	910	952	992	1,204	1,414	1,624	1,703	
30,000	188	406	656	706	756	806	856	906	956	1,006	1,056	1,106	1,156	1,406	1,656	1,906	2,000	50
	183	388	613	658	703	748	793	838	883	928	973	1,018	1,063	1,288	1,513	1,738	1,823	
32,000	200	433	700	753	807	860	913	967	1,020	1,073	1,127	1,180	1,233	1,500	1,767	2,033	2,133	53
	195	413	653	701	749	797	845	893	941	989	1,037	1,085	1,133	1,373	1,613	1,853	1,943	
34,000	213	460	744	800	857	914	970	1,027	1,084	1,140	1,197	1,254	1,310	1,594	1,877	2,160	2,267	56
	207	437	692	743	794	845	896	947	998	1,049	1,100	1,151	1,202	1,457	1,712	1,967	2,063	
36,000	225	488	788	848	908	968	1,028	1,088	1,148	1,208	1,268	1,328	1,388	1,688	1,988	2,288	2,400	60
	219	461	731	785	839	893	947	1,001	1,055	1,109	1,163	1,217	1,271	1,541	1,811	2,081	2,183	
38,000	238	515	831	895	958	1,021	1,085	1,148	1,211	1,275	1,338	1,401	1,465	1,781	2,098	2,415	2,533	63
	232	486	771	828	885	942	999	1,056	1,113	1,170	1,227	1,284	1,341	1,626	1,911	2,196	2,303	
40,000	250	542	875	942	1,008	1,075	1,142	1,208	1,275	1,342	1,408	1,475	1,542	1,875	2,208	2,542	2,667	66
	244	510	810	870	930	990	1,050	1,110	1,170	1,230	1,290	1,350	1,410	1,710	2,010	2,310	2,423	
42,000	263	569	919	989	1,059	1,129	1,199	1,269	1,339	1,409	1,479	1,549	1,619	1,969	2,319	2,669	2,800	70
	256	534	849	912	975	1,038	1,101	1,164	1,227	1,290	1,353	1,416	1,479	1,794	2,109	2,424	2,543	

Salary																		Years
44,000	275	596	963	1,036	1,109	1,183	1,256	1,329	1,403	1,476	1,549	1,623	1,696	2,063	2,429	2,796	2,933	73
	268	559	889	955	1,021	1,087	1,153	1,219	1,285	1,351	1,417	1,483	1,549	1,879	2,209	2,539	2,663	
46,000	288	623	1,006	1,083	1,160	1,236	1,313	1,390	1,466	1,543	1,620	1,696	1,773	2,156	2,540	2,923	3,067	76
	280	583	928	997	1,066	1,135	1,204	1,273	1,342	1,411	1,480	1,549	1,618	1,963	2,308	2,653	2,783	
48,000	300	650	1,050	1,130	1,210	1,290	1,370	1,450	1,530	1,610	1,690	1,770	1,850	2,250	2,650	3,050	3,200	80
	293	608	968	1,040	1,112	1,184	1,256	1,328	1,400	1,472	1,544	1,616	1,688	2,048	2,408	2,768	2,903	
50,000	313	677	1,094	1,177	1,260	1,344	1,427	1,510	1,594	1,677	1,760	1,844	1,927	2,344	2,760	3,177	3,333	83
	304	632	1,007	1,082	1,157	1,232	1,307	1,382	1,457	1,532	1,607	1,682	1,757	2,132	2,507	2,882	3,023	
53,000	331	718	1,159	1,248	1,336	1,424	1,513	1,601	1,689	1,778	1,866	1,954	2,043	2,484	2,926	3,368	3,533	88
	321	668	1,066	1,145	1,225	1,304	1,384	1,463	1,543	1,622	1,702	1,781	1,861	2,258	2,656	3,053	3,203	
55,000	344	745	1,203	1,295	1,386	1,478	1,570	1,661	1,753	1,845	1,936	2,028	2,120	2,578	3,036	3,495	3,667	91
	332	693	1,105	1,188	1,270	1,353	1,435	1,518	1,600	1,683	1,765	1,848	1,930	2,343	2,755	3,168	3,323	
57,000	356	772	1,247	1,342	1,437	1,532	1,627	1,722	1,817	1,912	2,007	2,102	2,197	2,672	3,147	3,622	3,800	95
	343	717	1,145	1,230	1,316	1,401	1,487	1,572	1,658	1,743	1,829	1,914	2,000	2,427	2,855	3,282	3,443	
60,000	375	813	1,313	1,413	1,513	1,613	1,713	1,813	1,913	2,013	2,113	2,213	2,313	2,813	3,313	3,813	4,000	100
	360	754	1,204	1,294	1,384	1,474	1,564	1,654	1,744	1,834	1,924	2,014	2,104	2,554	3,004	3,454	3,623	
65,000	406	880	1,422	1,530	1,639	1,747	1,855	1,964	2,072	2,180	2,289	2,397	2,505	3,047	3,589	4,130	4,333	108
	388	815	1,302	1,400	1,497	1,595	1,692	1,790	1,887	1,985	2,082	2,180	2,277	2,765	3,252	3,740	3,923	
66,000	413	894	1,444	1,554	1,664	1,774	1,884	1,994	2,104	2,214	2,324	2,434	2,544	3,094	3,644	4,194	4,400	110
	394	827	1,322	1,421	1,520	1,619	1,718	1,817	1,916	2,015	2,114	2,213	2,312	2,807	3,302	3,797	3,983	
68,000	425	921	1,488	1,601	1,714	1,828	1,941	2,054	2,168	2,281	2,394	2,508	2,621	3,188	3,754	4,321	4,533	113
	405	851	1,361	1,463	1,565	1,667	1,769	1,871	1,973	2,075	2,177	2,279	2,381	2,891	3,401	3,911	4,103	
70,000	438	948	1,531	1,648	1,765	1,881	1,998	2,115	2,231	2,348	2,465	2,581	2,698	3,281	3,865	4,448	4,667	116
	416	876	1,401	1,506	1,611	1,716	1,821	1,926	2,031	2,136	2,241	2,346	2,451	2,976	3,501	4,026	4,223	
72,000	450	975	1,575	1,695	1,815	1,935	2,055	2,175	2,295	2,415	2,535	2,655	2,775	3,375	3,975	4,575	4,800	120
	428	900	1,440	1,548	1,656	1,764	1,872	1,980	2,088	2,196	2,304	2,412	2,520	3,060	3,600	4,140	4,343	
74,000	463	1,002	1,619	1,742	1,865	1,989	2,112	2,235	2,359	2,482	2,605	2,729	2,852	3,469	4,085	4,702	4,933	123
	439	924	1,479	1,590	1,701	1,812	1,923	2,034	2,145	2,256	2,367	2,478	2,589	3,144	3,699	4,254	4,463	

Example illustrating computations: Assume an Average
Salary of $28,000 at 26 years of service:

For 1st 5 years use: 1 1/2% x $28,000 x 5 = $2,100.00
For 2nd 5 years use: 1 3/4% x $28,000 x 5 = 2,450.00
For balance of 16 years use: 2% x $28,000 x 16 = 8,960.00
Total annual annuity $13,510.00

The above figures are rounded to the nearest dollar

Divide by 12 (months) = $1,126 a month. If a survivor annuity is elected, the monthly annuity would be reduced to $1,036. If the above table does not cover your particular case, substitute exact figures to the formula of applicable example.
*For example, the monthly annuity for 26 years of service and an average salary of $28,000 is $1,079 plus $46, or $1,125.

FEDERAL EMPLOYEES' RETIREMENT SYSTEM (FERS) TABLE
Monthly Basic Annuity Amounts Based on "High-3" Salary And Years of Service For Employees
(Second line of each salary level reflects annuity with survivor deduction.)

Highest 3 Year Average Salary	YEARS OF CREDITABLE SERVICE																	Amounts For Each Add'l Yr. Unlisted*
	5	10	15	16	17	18	19	20	21	22	23	24	25	30	35	40	42	
20,000	83	167	250	267	283	300	317	333	350	367	383	400	417	500	583	667	700	16
	75	150	225	240	255	270	285	300	315	330	345	360	375	450	525	600	630	
22,000	92	183	275	293	312	330	348	367	385	403	422	440	458	550	642	733	770	18
	83	165	248	264	281	297	314	330	347	363	380	396	413	495	578	660	693	
24,000	100	200	300	320	340	360	380	400	420	440	460	480	500	600	700	800	840	20
	90	180	270	288	306	324	342	360	378	396	414	432	450	540	630	720	756	
26,000	108	217	325	347	368	390	412	433	455	477	498	520	542	650	758	867	910	21
	98	195	293	312	332	351	371	390	410	429	449	468	488	585	683	780	819	
28,000	117	233	350	373	397	420	443	467	490	513	537	560	583	700	817	933	980	23
	105	210	315	336	357	378	399	420	441	462	483	504	525	630	735	840	882	
30,000	125	250	375	400	425	450	475	500	525	550	575	600	625	750	875	1,000	1,050	25
	113	225	338	360	383	405	428	450	473	495	518	540	563	675	788	900	945	
32,000	133	267	400	427	453	480	507	533	560	587	613	640	667	800	933	1,067	1,120	26
	120	240	360	384	408	432	456	480	504	528	552	576	600	720	840	960	1,008	
34,000	142	283	425	453	482	510	538	567	595	623	652	680	708	850	992	1,133	1,190	28
	128	255	383	408	434	459	485	510	536	561	587	612	638	765	893	1,020	1,071	
36,000	150	300	450	480	510	540	570	600	630	660	690	720	750	900	1,050	1,200	1,260	30
	135	270	405	432	459	486	513	540	567	594	621	648	675	810	945	1,080	1,134	
38,000	158	317	475	507	538	570	602	633	665	697	728	760	792	950	1,108	1,267	1,330	31
	143	285	428	456	485	513	542	570	599	627	656	684	713	855	998	1,140	1,197	
40,000	167	333	500	533	567	600	633	667	700	733	767	800	833	1,000	1,167	1,333	1,400	33
	150	300	450	480	510	540	570	600	630	660	690	720	750	900	1,050	1,200	1,260	
42,000	175	350	525	560	595	630	665	700	735	770	805	840	875	1,050	1,225	1,400	1,470	35
	158	315	473	504	536	567	599	630	662	693	725	756	788	945	1,103	1,260	1,323	

Salary																		
44,000	183	367	550	587	623	660	697	733	770	807	843	880	917	1,100	1,283	1,467	1,540	36
	165	330	495	528	561	594	627	660	693	726	759	792	825	990	1,155	1,320	1,386	
46,000	192	383	575	613	652	690	728	767	805	843	882	920	958	1,150	1,342	1,533	1,610	38
	173	345	518	552	587	621	656	690	725	759	794	828	863	1,035	1,208	1,380	1,449	
48,000	200	400	600	640	680	720	760	800	840	880	920	960	1,000	1,200	1,400	1,600	1,680	40
	180	360	540	576	612	648	684	720	756	792	828	864	900	1,080	1,260	1,440	1,512	
50,000	208	417	625	667	708	750	792	833	875	917	958	1,000	1,042	1,250	1,458	1,667	1,750	41
	188	375	563	600	638	675	713	750	788	825	863	900	938	1,125	1,313	1,500	1,575	
53,000	221	442	663	707	751	795	839	883	928	972	1,016	1,060	1,104	1,325	1,546	1,767	1,855	44
	199	398	596	636	676	716	755	795	835	875	914	954	994	1,193	1,391	1,590	1,670	
55,000	229	458	688	733	779	825	871	917	963	1,008	1,054	1,100	1,146	1,375	1,604	1,833	1,925	45
	206	413	619	660	701	743	784	825	866	908	949	990	1,031	1,238	1,444	1,650	1,733	
57,000	238	475	713	760	808	855	903	950	998	1,045	1,093	1,140	1,188	1,425	1,663	1,900	1,995	47
	214	428	641	684	727	770	812	855	898	941	983	1,026	1,069	1,283	1,496	1,710	1,796	
60,000	250	500	750	800	850	900	950	1,000	1,050	1,100	1,150	1,200	1,250	1,500	1,750	2,000	2,100	50
	225	450	675	720	765	810	855	900	945	990	1,035	1,080	1,125	1,350	1,575	1,800	1,890	
65,000	271	542	813	867	921	975	1,029	1,083	1,138	1,192	1,246	1,300	1,354	1,625	1,896	2,167	2,275	54
	244	488	731	780	829	878	926	975	1,024	1,073	1,121	1,170	1,219	1,463	1,706	1,950	2,048	
66,000	275	550	825	880	935	990	1,045	1,100	1,155	1,210	1,265	1,320	1,375	1,650	1,925	2,200	2,310	55
	248	495	743	792	842	891	941	990	1,040	1,089	1,139	1,188	1,238	1,485	1,733	1,980	2,079	
68,000	283	567	850	907	963	1,020	1,077	1,133	1,190	1,247	1,303	1,360	1,417	1,700	1,983	2,267	2,380	56
	255	510	765	816	867	918	969	1,020	1,071	1,122	1,173	1,224	1,275	1,530	1,785	2,040	2,142	
70,000	292	583	875	933	992	1,050	1,108	1,167	1,225	1,283	1,342	1,400	1,458	1,750	2,042	2,333	2,450	58
	-263	525	788	840	893	945	998	1,050	1,103	1,155	1,208	1,260	1,313	1,575	1,838	2,100	2,205	
72,000	300	600	900	960	1,020	1,080	1,140	1,200	1,260	1,320	1,380	1,440	1,500	1,800	2,100	2,400	2,520	60
	270	540	810	864	918	972	1,026	1,080	1,134	1,188	1,242	1,296	1,350	1,620	1,890	2,160	2,268	
74,000	308	617	925	987	1,048	1,110	1,172	1,233	1,295	1,357	1,418	1,480	1,542	1,850	2,158	2,467	2,590	61
	278	555	833	888	944	999	1,055	1,110	1,166	1,221	1,277	1,332	1,388	1,665	1,943	2,220	2,331	

Example illustrating an average annual salary at 30 years of service: 1% of $32,000 = $320, times 30 (years of service) = $9,600 annual annuity or $800 monthly. If the employee opted at retirement to elect a survivor annuity, his monthly annuity would be reduced by 10% to $720. (Employees who continue to serve at age 62 or older with 20 years of service will have their annuity computed at 1.1 percent. For example, the same employee in the example above who retires at age 62 or older would have an annual annuity of $10,560 or $880 monthly. If a survivor annuity is elected, the monthly annuity would be $792).

*For example, the monthly annuity for 26 years of service and an average salary of $26,000 is $542 plus $21, or $563 per month.

(Continued from page 71)

deceased child distributed among the descendants of that child;

Fourth: if none of the above, to your parents (or parent);

Fifth: if none of the above, to the executor or administrator of your estate;

Sixth: if none of the above, to your next of kin who may be entitled under the laws of the state in which you are domiciled at the time of your death.

4. *Designation of Beneficiary.* You do not need to designate a beneficiary to receive the lump-sum death benefit unless you wish to name a person or persons not mentioned in the order of precedence shown in item *To Whom Payable* above, or unless you wish to name a person who is mentioned but in a different order or for a different share. A designation of beneficiary is for lump-sum death benefit purposes only and does not affect the right of any person who can qualify for a survivor annuity. A designation of beneficiary must be in writing (Standard Form 2808 is provided for this purpose) and must be received in the Office of Personnel Management before your death. If you designate a beneficiary, remember to keep your designation current. Changes in your family or employment status without a corresponding change in your designation may result in a settlement other than you intended.

ANNUITY REDUCTIONS FOR EMPLOYEES WITHOUT SPOUSES*

Age of Person Named in Relation to That of Retiring Employee	*Reduction in Annuity of Retiring Employee*
Older, same age, or less than 5 years younger	10%
5 but less than 10 years younger	15%
10 but less than 15 years younger	20%
15 but less than 20 years younger	25%
20 but less than 25 years younger	30%
25 but less than 30 years younger	35%
30 or more years younger	40%

* Both FERS and CSRS

CHAPTER 7
TO MOVE OR NOT TO MOVE

There's no place like home. Unfortunately, that is what many postal and federal retirees discover when they pick up their first retirement checks and head for warmer climates.

Moving before you have assessed all of the pros and cons of shifting to a new location can be an expensive mistake.

In this chapter we look at some of the factors you might want to consider before you begin packing. We will explore financial, emotional, cultural, medical and other considerations. Put a plus in the allotted space after each section which you believe argues for the move. Place a minus in the space after each section you believe argues against the move. Count the number of plus and minus checks. If there are more plus signs, a move may be right for you. If there are more minus signs, you'd better look again before putting up that "for sale" sign.

- **Financial.** Have you compared the cost of housing in the area in which you retire to the cost in a new area? The difference can be substantial. The difference can work both ways. For instance, if you retire in Washington, D.C., and move to one of the farm states, you probably could sell your house in Washington for considerably more than you will have to pay for a house in Iowa. If, on the other hand, you sell your house in Iowa and plan to buy one in San Francisco, you will receive a shock greater than that experienced in the recent earthquake.

  In your situation, is this a _____ plus or a _____ minus?

  Would it be possible for you to rent your current home while you are spending time exploring the new area? Perhaps you can arrange a "house swap" for a couple of months with someone in the area to which you are planning to relocate. Some couples find this an ideal way to get an inexpensive vacation. The furnishings in both your house and the house to which you are moving would remain unchanged during the "swap" period. At the end of the agreed time the couples could simply switch back to their original residences. Each would have a better idea of what life would be like in a new area.

In your situation, is this a ＿＿＿ plus or a ＿＿＿ minus?

Do you have sufficient funds laid aside to cover the cost of an exploratory trip to the new area? Have you realistically calculated how much you will have to spend for food and temporary shelter while you look for permanent housing in the new area?

In your situation, is this a ＿＿＿ plus or a ＿＿＿ minus?

As you consider moving, have you and your spouse thoroughly discussed the kind of housing you want in the new area? The financial differences between buying a single family house, a townhouse or a condominium can be enormous. One spouse may long for a penthouse suite while the other wants nothing higher than two stories.

In your situation, is this a ＿＿＿ plus or a ＿＿＿ minus?

Have you checked the cost of moving your furniture to a new location? Over the years you probably have accumulated a substantial amount of furniture. The cost of moving it to another area, particularly a distant one, may provide you with a rude awakening from your retirement dream.

You can avoid this by contacting long distance moving companies for an estimate. Some companies have booklets showing you how to calculate moving costs. They also offer tips on packing your household goods yourself and saving some moving costs.

There are other options. You can rent a truck and get your friends and relatives to help you move. This will cut the cost. You can take a close look at your furniture and decide whether it is worth the cost of moving. A word of caution. Don't underestimate the value of what you have. It could cost thousands of dollars to replace that dining room or bedroom set or even that old piano. Items you take for granted, like sofas, bookcases, coffee tables, VCRs and other electronic entertainment units quickly add up to a large amount when you think about replacing them.

In your situation, is this a _____ plus or a _____ minus?

- **Emotional**. Do you have close emotional ties to the area in which you now live? Are you or your spouse active in civic, school and church activities? Are you really ready to pull up stakes and move, possibly thousands of miles, from the grandchildren? What about the bridge parties, the bingo games, the neighborhood barbecues? Have you become to depend on nearby friends or relatives for help when you have an emergency? Will you be uncomfortable without such support contacts?

Are you sure you have taken into consideration the needs of both spouses? It is too easy to have all of the plans based on the needs of one spouse simply because he or she was the breadwinner in the family. Sometimes something so simple as the lack of an opportunity to have a garden can turn one spouse against moving.

In your situation, is this a _____ plus or a _____ minus?

- **Cultural.** Is there an opportunity to pursue cultural activities in the new area? If you like concerts, operas, stage shows, dinner theaters or drive-in movies, will you find them in the new area? There is an easy way to find out. Send for a newspaper from the nearest big city as well as one from the town to which you are considering relocating.

Check out the available entertainment. Do they have branches of social groups in which you are interested? If the city is in a coastal area, do they have fishing boats or cruise ships? If you are looking at a smaller town, does it have golf courses or tennis courts?

If you want to combine the cultural activities of the big city with the comfort of a small town, consider moving to a college town. This could be a particularly wise move if you have dependents to educate or if you want to pursue further studies on your own. Being a property owner in the town might allow you to attend the school at lower rates than non-residents. You would, of course, want to find out about the housing availability and cost in the area to which you are considering moving.

Be aware of tourist areas with seasonal appeal. You may like the bustling activity during the "in season," but might find most of the activities closed down when the season ends.

In your situation, is this a _____ plus or a _____ minus?

- **Medical.** As you enter your retirement years you are more likely to suffer a variety of ailments that go with the aging process. How will the medical facilities in the new area compare with those you now use? Are you likely to need the services of a cardiologist or some other medical specialist to treat existing conditions? Are there good hospitals and medical facilities nearby? If you are entitled to benefits as the result of military service, are there bases nearby with good hospitals? Can you find satisfactory medical facilities and care in the new area?

You can get help in answering this question by consulting your current care providers. They frequently can recommend a colleague in the new area or at least refer you to someone in the local medical society. Dentists, surgeons, chiropractors, podiatrists or any other medical specialists can advise you on available medical care in your new homesite.

Will your health insurance plan be acceptable in the new area? If you are dealing with a Health Maintenance Organization (HMO) it is quite possible that it would not have facilities in the area to which you are moving.

In your situation, is this a _____ plus or a _____ minus?

Once you have focused on an area and have enough data to convince you that you might want to move, look again at the financial factors. What taxes are levied on residents?

Is there a state income tax? Is a sales tax imposed by the state or locality or both? (See table at end of this chapter). Does the state or locality have a personal property tax? Are annuity benefits taxed? The chart in chapter 4 will help you answer that question. Is there a homestead exemption putting a smaller tax burden on permanent residents than applies to seasonal visitors?

Does the area have a heavy population of young people? This could cause school taxes to be high.

What licenses are needed to use your car, go hunting or take a fishing trip?

Does the state have special benefits for retirees? (For example, exemptions from certain license fees, free admission to state parks, and reduced fees for using some state programs). Some states devote income from state lotteries to the care of the elderly.

In your situation is this a _____ plus or a _____ minus?

Add up your plusses and minuses and you have a good indication of which way you should go.

Don't overlook demographics. Is the town to which you are going populated mostly by older people? It might be a quieter placed to live, but it could be too quiet. It gets to be a sad situation when you look out in the park and see only older people looking for names of friends in the obituary column.

Conversely, you might be one of those people who are perpetually young and will find happiness in a community populated mainly by youth. These people are easy to spot. They look and act as if they just came off a cruise ship.

Ideally, you want a mix of all age groups. Being part of a family-oriented community gives you an opportunity to enjoy the youngsters during the day and retreating to your quiet house at night.

How do you compare the communities in which you might want to live? You can find out more about them by writing to the Chamber of Commerce, the local newspaper, the library or the elected city officials. Maps and tour books available from groups like the American Automobile Association also give thumbnail sketches of the area. If you are looking at a college town, the school will be happy to send you scads of information.

Make a game of researching potential retirement areas. You

and your spouse will have fun and get a great geography lesson
in the process.

TAX CHANGES EFFECTIVE IN 1990, 1991, AND 1992

State	Sales Tax[1] Rate	Income Taxes[2] In Effect (X=Yes)	Income Taxes[2] Maximum Rate	Fuel Taxes[3] Gasoline (Rate Per Gallon)	Fuel Taxes[3] Diesel Fuel (Rate Per Gallon)
Alabama	4.00%	X	5.00%	11.00¢	12.00¢
Alaska	—	—	—	8.00¢	8.00¢
Arizona	5.00%	X	8.00%	17.00¢	17.00¢
Arkansas	4.00%	X	7.00%	13.50¢	12.50¢
California	5.00%	X	9.30%	9.00¢	9.00¢
Colorado	3.00%	X	5.00%	20.00¢	20.50¢
Connecticut	8.00%	—	—	22.00¢	22.00¢
Delaware	—	X	7.70%	16.00¢	16.00¢
Dist. of Columbia	6.00%	X	9.50%	18.00¢	18.00¢
Florida	6.00%	—	—	4.00¢	4.00¢
Georgia	4.00%	X	6.00%	7.50¢	7.50¢
Hawaii	4.00%	X	10.00%		
Hawaii County				19.80¢	19.80¢
Honolulu County				27.50¢	27.50¢
Kauai County				21.00¢	21.00¢
Maui County				20.00¢	20.00¢
Idaho	5.00%	X	8.20%	19.00¢	19.00¢
Illinois	6.25%	X	2.50%	19.00¢	21.50¢
Indiana	5.00%	X	3.40%	15.00¢	16.00¢
Iowa	4.00%	X	9.98%	20.00¢	22.50¢
Kansas	4.25%	X	8.75%	16.00¢	18.00¢
Kentucky	6.00%	X	6.00%	15.00¢	12.00¢
Louisiana	4.00%	X	6.00%	20.00¢	20.00¢
Maine	5.00%	X	8.50%	17.00¢	20.00¢
Maryland	5.00%	X	5.00%	18.50¢	18.50¢
Massachusetts	5.00%	X	5.375%	17.00¢	17.00¢
Michigan	4.00%	X	4.60%	15.00¢	15.00¢
Minnesota	6.00%	X	8.50%	20.00¢	20.00¢
Mississippi	6.00%	X	5.00%	18.00¢	18.00¢
Missouri	4.225%	X	6.00%	11.00¢	11.00¢
Montana	—	X	11.00%	20.00¢	20.00¢
Nebraska	5.00%	X	5.90%	21.90¢	21.90¢
Nevada	5.75%	—	—	16.25¢	22.00¢

State	Sales Tax[1] Rate	In Effect (X=Yes)	Income Taxes[2] Maximum Rate	Fuel Taxes[3] Gasoline (Rate Per Gallon)	Diesel Fuel (Rate Per Gallon)
New Hampshire	—	—	—	16.00¢	16.00¢
New Jersey	7.00%	X	3.50%	10.50¢	13.50¢
New Mexico	5.00%	X	8.50%	16.20¢	16.20¢
New York	4.00%	X	7.875%	8.00¢	10.00¢
North Carolina	3.00%	X	7.00%	21.50¢	21.50¢
North Dakota	5.00%	X	14.00%	17.00¢	17.00¢
Ohio	5.00%	X	6.90%	20.00¢	20.00¢
Oklahoma	4.00%	X	10.00%	16.00¢	13.00¢
Oregon	—	X	9.00%	18.00¢	18.00¢
Pennsylvania	6.00%	X	2.10%	12.00¢	12.00¢
Rhode Island	7.00%	X	—	20.00¢	20.00¢
South Carolina	5.00%	X	7.00%	16.00¢	16.00¢
South Dakota	4.00%	—	—	18.00¢	18.00¢
Tennessee	5.50%	—	—	20.00¢	17.00¢
Texas	6.25%	—	—	15.00¢	15.00¢
Utah	5.00%	X	7.20%	19.00¢	19.00¢
Vermont	4.00%	X	—	15.00¢	16.00¢
Virginia	3.50%	X	5.75%	17.50¢	16.00¢
Washington	6.50%	—	—	22.00¢	22.00¢
West Virginia	6.00%	X	6.50%	15.50¢	15.50¢
Wisconsin	5.00%	X	6.93%	21.50¢	21.50¢
Wyoming	3.00%	—	—	9.00¢	9.00¢

FOOTNOTES

SALES TAXES

[1] Local tax rates are additional.

California: Rate reduced to 4-3/4% on January 1, 1991.

Missouri: Rate reduced to 4-1/8% on July 1, 1990.

Nevada: Tax rate is a composite of a 2% state rate plus a 3-3/4% state-mandated county rate.

Rhode Island: Rate reduced to 6.5% on July 1, 1991, and to 6% on July 1, 1992.

INCOME TAXES

[2] Income tax rates do not include local rates. All states with income taxes require withholding from residents.

Colorado: Alternative minimum tax imposed.

Connecticut: Taxes capital gains (7%) and dividends and interest (1% - 14%).

Illinois: Tax rate is 3% from July 1, 1989 through June 30, 1991.

Massachusetts: Taxes earned income. Massachusetts source interest and annuities (5%) and other interest, dividends, and capital gains (10%, 5%, and 5.75%, respectively, for 1990; 10% after 1990).

New Hampshire: Taxes interest and dividends (5%).

Rhode Island: 22.96% of modified federal income tax.

Tennessee: Taxes only dividends and interest (6%).

Vermont: 25% of federal income tax.

GASOLINE/DIESEL FUEL TAXES

[3] Local tax rates are additional.

Arizona: Tax increased to 18¢ per gallon on October 1, 1990.

Colorado: The gasoline tax rate is reduced to 22¢ per gallon for calendar years beginning on January 1, 1991. The special fuel tax rate is reduced to 18¢ per gallon during 1990 and 1991 and is increased to 20.5¢ per gallon on January 1, 1992.

Connecticut: The tax rates are increased to 22¢ on July 1, 1990, and 23¢ on July 1, 1991.

Delaware: Rate increases to 19¢ per gallon on January 1, 1991.

Georgia: An additional tax is levied at the rate of 3% of the retail sale price.

Hawaii: Rates are combined state and county rates.

Illinois: An additional tax is imposed on special fuel used by commercial motor vehicles, based on the average selling price of special fuel sold in the state. Until January 1, 1993, an additional 3¢ -per-gallon tax is imposed on receivers of motor fuel, aviation fuels, and home heating oil and kerosene, but excluding liquified petroleum gases.

Kansas: The gasoline tax rate is increased to 17¢ per gallon on July 1, 1991, and to 18¢ per gallon on July 1, 1992. The diesel fuel tax rates are increased to 19¢ per gallon on July 1, 1991, and to 20¢ per gallon on July 1, 1992.

Mississippi: The gasoline tax rate will be reduced to 14.4¢ per gallon and the diesel tax rate reduced to 14.75¢ per gallon on September 1, 2001.

Nevada: An additional tax will be levied if the federal tax on fuel is reduced or discontinued. The additional tax will be equal to the federal tax reduction, but not to exceed 4¢ per gallon.

Oregon: The rate increased to 20¢ per gallon on January 1, 1991.

Tennessee: Plus an additional 1¢ per gallon special petroleum products tax.

Vermont: Tax reduced by 1¢ per gallon on April 1, 1991. Licensed users pay diesel fuel tax rate for vehicles of less than 10,000 pounds, and 25¢ per gallon for vehicles weighing greater than 10,000 pounds.

Washington: The tax rates are increased to 23¢ effective April 1, 1991.

CHAPTER 8
A SPOUSE IN THE HOUSE

When men or women retire they look forward to enjoying their new status. They will have more time to spend with their mates, lots of free time and an opportunity to do some traveling. The children are out of college or soon will be, the house is almost paid for and the monthly annuity check leaves a few bucks to spend on recreation. Just Molly and me in my blue heaven.

Sounds idyllic. Right? Maybe! Suppose the other occupant in that heaven is a spouse for whom your retirement could mean a disruption of the routine into which he or she has comfortably settled? Remember, the whole world isn't retiring, just you!

Perhaps the best advice at this point is don't retire until you have something to do. This doesn't mean you have to get a full schedule of volunteer work, gardening and a batch of other projects to fill your available time. It does mean that you need an excuse for getting up in the morning. Without it you will quickly age into a fat couch potato wrinkled up in front of the TV.

Since the decision to retire probably isn't made on the spur of the moment, retirement planning should include discussions with your spouse about what life would be like after you retire.

It is important to remember that retirement is not always a family affair. Just because one working spouse retires it doesn't mean the other will retire at the same time.

There are a number of reasons why it may not be practical to retire at the same time. These include:

- An age difference between the spouses, with the younger spouse not yet eligible for retirement.

- Retirement of both spouses might deplete the family finances. This could be a problem, especially if the family has children at or near college age and cannot afford the cost if their income is lowered substantially. It also could be true if there is need to provide financial aid to an elderly relative needing medical care or transfer to a retirement community.

- The spouse who is not retiring may not be psychologically ready to retire. He or she may enjoy the job, the prestige and the income it provides. Be sure to consider this aspect before urging your spouse to retire at the same time you do. Unless you both have definite plans as to how and where you will spend your retirement years, it might be best for the one spouse to continue working a while longer.

Whether your spouse is working or retired, this is the time to develop some kind of routine and build your day around it. Don't forget your spouse already has a daily routine and might not be comfortable trying to fit into your plans. Remember that he or she probably has special interests and wants to continue them.

Don't expect your spouse to change to accommodate your plans. It is just like a marriage where the bride figures that whatever flaws she finds in her mate will disappear once they are married and she straightens him out. The divorce courts are filled with people who found it doesn't work that way.

Let your spouse continue to play his or her own role. Remember you are now dealing with a situation in which the household has about half the income and twice the mate. Neither spouse wants the other to suddenly attempt to inject management skills or budget planning tactics into an area which, up to now, has been the exclusive domain of one or the other. We interviewed the wife of a government executive. Her spouse is within three years of retirement and she dreads the day when he will be all hers, all of the time.

She told us: "I'm afraid I won't be able to live my own life because I will be even more wrapped up in his life than I am now. We now have breakfast and dinner together. Throwing in lunch may be more than I can handle."

Her concern increases when she looks at neighborhood families where the breadwinner has retired. She says some of them seemed to have aged overnight because they no longer had a purpose for living. She noted that some of the wives went out and got part time jobs because they "had no life of their own." The same would be true if the wife were the retiree.

Money—or the lack of it—was cited as the major retirement concern among many of the potential retirees we interviewed. If all of your working years were spent in a federal government job, you may not have made many outside investments to supplement your retirement income.

The thrift plans and other programs will ease this problem in future years, but this is of little help to people who have only a couple of years to go before retirement. Many were at the top of their grades during the last few years on the job and qualified for only the cost-of-living raises voted by the Congress. As they ponder retirement they wonder if they will be financially pinched in later years. It is a legitimate concern.

Many people due to retire in the next few years are in the "sandwich generation." They are sandwiched between being young enough to still have children in college while also having to worry about aging parents.

Since Biblical times we have heard the philosophy that children will grow up to take care of their aging parents. In some societies this is a given and it is not uncommon to have two or three generations living under one roof. Now we wonder as we hear about a mother who was able to take care of seven kids but now the seven kids are unable to take care of one mother.

Dealing with aging, both your own and that of those near and dear to you is not easy. You never know when you will be called upon to assist an elderly relative or start raising a new family because one of your chicks turned out to be a homing pigeon and now is back in the nest with a couple of young ones.

People are living longer these days. Medical science has made marvelous strides in slowing the aging process. That is a happy thought except for the realization that the life may last longer than the resources.

Many retired couples find this a good time to explore possible sources of additional income. This not only provides for a more active existence, it provides the comfort of knowing you can pay when the bills come due. Elsewhere in this book we discuss ways to turn hobbies or part-time activities into added income.

If you planned your investments carefully you may not need to work after retirement. This is not to say you shouldn't work, but you should have enough funds to be able to stay home and do nothing if that is your goal in retirement.

Perhaps you don't need the money but you still want some useful activity in your life. This opens the door to both spouses to get into some volunteer activity. A hospital is one place where each of you can find satisfying projects.

There are many jobs to be done and the hospital staff will be happy to work with you to find the one most satisfying to you. The same is true in working with other service organizations.

> *"People are living longer these days. Medical science has made marvelous strides in slowing the aging process. That is a happy thought except for the realization that the life may last longer than the resources."*

The type of volunteer work you do should be determined by your personality and interests.

Volunteer work is very rewarding. Being around people less fortunate than we are makes it easier to accept our own problems, or at least to see them in a better perspective.

Perhaps you or your spouse are more geared to less formal activities or commitments. Think of all the lonely kids out there who would love to have a foster grandparent to visit with and share secrets and love.

If you have trouble locating such children just check with your church or charitable organization. There are many agencies that would be delighted to give you names of families that could use your help. Help to such families doesn't necessarily mean money— although a few extra dollars are always helpful. The help can be nothing more than a friendly conversation and a little bit of your time.

An ideal project for individuals or couples is the literacy program offered in many areas. What a thrill to know you opened up a new life for someone by teaching them to read and write.

Be assured that there are volunteer programs available that will accommodate whatever amount of time you are able to give to them. The Red Cross can use your help in its blood donor programs. "Meals on Wheels" programs need volunteers both to prepare and deliver the meals. Girl and Boy Scout troops need leaders at all levels. Crisis intervention programs will train you how to respond to calls from desperate and disturbed individuals. It is not uncommon for such volunteer work to result in saving lives.

If your interest is in animals rather than people, your local humane society will welcome any help you are willing to provide.

Travel and convention centers are eager to recruit volunteers, particularly those with knowledge of a foreign language. These volunteers often work at railroad terminals or airports helping confused travelers get safely on their way.

In researching this book we talked with many retirees and their spouses. We asked them what difference they expected retirement to make in their lives. By far the most common answer was the need for each of the partners to retain his or her individuality.

A nurse at one of the agencies we visited told us: "Retirement is not a time when you have to do everything together. Your interests may be very different than those of your spouse." She told us: "I don't think God meant for a man and a woman to be together under the same roof for 24 hours of every day. I think a man back in the house full time disrupts the routine. It is easy for the wife in such cases to develop the attitude that many of her chores can wait until tomorrow because she sees her husband sitting around reading the paper."

One retired woman told us she gets up each morning and dresses as if she still were going to the office. She even puts on her make-up and then does her household chores.

None of these comments are meant to discourage retirement. It can be a wonderful and happy time of your life if you sprinkle your planning with a good measure of common sense.

You can still travel although you might not be able to do it as often or with as fancy accommodations. This is a time when wise couples will sit down and plan their vacations and other trips. By carefully studying what is available they learn that it is possible to save a good deal of money by traveling at times other than the height of the "season."

Anyone who has spent time in the southern vacation belt knows that May or September are wonderful months to visit. And, since those are off-season months, the rates are much lower than what they are normally. Add that to the discounts for which you can qualify as senior citizens and you'll have a happy and less expensive time.

You may not be able to afford the most expensive items on the menu when you eat out. Savor the company in which you are enjoying the meal. This approach can make a simple meal seem like a banquet. Finding joy in simple pleasures is what happy retirement is all about. You'll find it because you have more time to look!

CHAPTER 10
A PENNY SAVED

The Thrift Savings Plan (TSP) is a retirement savings and investment plan for employees of the federal government and the U.S. Postal Service. Congress established the plan in the Federal Employees' Retirement System Act of 1986. The plan offers federal and Postal Service civilian employees many of the savings and tax benefits private corporations offer their employees.

Public Law 101-335, passed in mid-1990, liberalizes the options and broadens the eligibility for participation in the thrift plan. It also:

- authorizes employing agencies to use their appropriated funds to pay lost earnings into the accounts of TSP participants who lost those earnings due to certain employing agency error;

- removes the restrictions relating to contributions in the C and F Funds;

- exempts the purchase of Thrift Plan annuities from state and local premium taxes;

- clarifies the distinction between the date an annuity is purchased and the date the annuity commences; and,

- authorizes the Board to make cash payments to employees with a final Thrift Savings Account balance of $3,500 or less who do not select one of the other available withdrawal options.

The Federal Retirement Thrift Investment Board, the independent agency which administers the TSP, will be revising its publications to reflect the new changes in the law. A revised *Summary of the Thrift Savings Plans for Federal Employees* and *TSP Update* will be available in your government personnel offices when the new benefits are available.

PARTICIPATION

The Thrift Savings Plan is open to federal and postal employees covered by FERS, CSRS, and other equivalent government retirement plans. Generally, FERS employees are those hired on or after January 1, 1984, while CSRS employees are those hired before that date who did not convert to FERS. There are different participation rules for each group.

Benefits earned under the plan are in addition to the CSRS and FERS defined benefit annuities. TSP is a **defined contribution** plan administered by the Federal Retirement Thrift Investment Board. This means the benefits you derive from the plan will depend on the amount of contributions made by you and your agency. It also depends on the earnings on those contributions and the method you choose to withdraw your account balance.

The Thrift Plan makes it possible for employees to increase their retirement nest egg substantially when their contributions are added to the government contributions and earnings on investment of the funds.

The amount you and your agency may contribute is set by law. The contributions you make to your TSP account are voluntary and separate from your contribution to CSRS or FERS. FERS employees receive automatic contributions from their agencies as well as matching contributions based on the amount they contribute each pay period.

The 1990 law removes the restrictions on the way FERS participants may allocate their investments among the various funds in the Thrift Savings Plan. The old law required that specified portions of contributions be invested in the Government Securities Investment Fund (G Fund) over a 10-year period.

The new law eliminated the investment fund restrictions on contributions of both FERS and CSRS covered employees.

Both the Congressional Budget Office and the Office of Management and Budget have concluded that investments in the TSP qualify as "non-budget" items. Since the Plan investments and the moving around of funds will have no budgetary impact, the lawmakers felt there was no reason to retain the investment restrictions.

Your agency reports information about you and your TSP contributions to the U.S. Department of Agriculture's National Finance Center (NFC) in New Orleans, Louisiana, which maintains records of your participation. It also provides certain limited services such as withdrawals, loans, and interfund transfers. However, all of your questions about the plan and your participation in it should be directed to your personnel office.

CSRS

The CSRS savings plan became effective April 1, 1987. It:

- offers a combination of benefits that give a tax break for today and a savings plan for the future.

- allows CSRS employees to contribute up to 5 percent of basic pay per pay period. CSRS employees do not receive any agency matching or agency automatic contributions.

- requires continuation of the 7 percent of salary that employees already contribute to the CSRS retirement fund.

FERS

The rules are different for FERS employees who want to participate in the Thrift Savings Plan. They may:

- contribute up to 10 percent of their basic pay per pay period to the plan. Federal tax law sets an upper limit on contributions which is adjusted annually by the Internal Revenue Service. Your personnel office will notify you if you reach the investment limit.

- receive agency matching contributions of up to 4 percent of their basic pay contributed each pay period. The agency matches dollar for dollar the first 3 percent of pay contributed, and 50 cents on the dollar for the next 2 percent.

- receive agency automatic (1 percent) contributions whether or not they contribute to their TSP accounts.

You get an additional tax break under the savings plans because the money comes out of your pay before federal and, in most cases, state or local income taxes are computed. You will have to pay the taxes when you withdraw the money. But, you should be in a lower tax bracket by that time and thus pay less taxes than you would if the money were part of your current income.

Some independent government agencies, such as the financial industry regulators, offer 401-K retirement savings plans under which they match a certain portion of contributions by employees. Money put into the 401-K plans offers the option of investment in funds other than government securities.

> *"You will have to pay the taxes when you withdraw the money. But, you should be in a lower tax bracket by that time and thus pay less taxes than you would if the money were part of your current income."*

Note that CSRS participants are covered by the same maximum annual contribution limit (in 1991, $8,475) which applies to FERS and that all contributions must be made through payroll deduction.

Several factors will determine how big your savings bundle will be. These include your salary, how much you save and for how long, and how well the funds in which you elect to invest pan out.

The law contains a specific definition of basic pay for computing thrift plan contributions. For most employees, basic pay is the same as gross salary earned. For re-employed annuitants the basic pay for TSP purposes is the basic pay of record; it is not reduced by the amount of the participant's annuity. Your personnel office can clarify any questions you may have about basic pay computation.

As noted earlier, the government automatically sets up a Thrift Plan for FERS employees when they become eligible to contribute to the TSP. It begins with an agency automatic contribution whereby the government contributes an amount equal to 1 percent of your pay every pay period. You do not have to make any contribution to receive this payment.

In addition to the basic contribution, you will have an opportunity to contribute up to 10 percent of your basic pay to the fund and receive additional agency matching contributions from the government.

The following chart shows how the government matches contributions by employees in the FERS thrift program:

If you save	The government will add	Total
0%	1.0% (automatic)	1.0%
1%	2.0%	3.0%
2%	3.0%	5.0%
3%	4.0%	7.0%
4%	4.5%	8.5%
5%	5.0%	10.0 %
6%-10%	(maximum)	11-15%

All of the money in your Thrift Savings Plan Account, except for the 1 percent contributed by the government, belongs to you as soon as it gets into the account. The 1 percent government contribution belongs to you after you have worked for the government for three years.

The money in your Thrift Savings Plan account can be invested in any of three different funds. The 1990 law also removes the statutory restrictions on investments made by participants covered by CSRS. Prior to the 1990 law, CSRS participants could only invest in the G Fund. The new law allows all participants the option of investing in any or all of the funds.

If you are retired or about to retire, you might want to consider investing in the more conservative funds. This is especially true if you are operating on a tight budget and can't afford to have large fluctuations in your investment income.

The Thrift Savings Plan is designed to be held for a long time. That is why you cannot withdraw your account while you are still employed by the federal government. However, you may borrow certain funds in the account under limited circumstances. Conditions under which loans are allowed are detailed later in this chapter.

If you leave government service before qualifying for retirement, you can withdraw only the amount in which you are vested.

BENEFITS

The thrift plan, even with its minor restrictions on vesting, provides a new freedom of investment and retirement planning for federal and postal employees. It accepts the fact that many employees may not want to spend their entire working life in a federal government job. Realizing this, the government benefits were made "portable" so employees who left early will have a base upon which to build a retirement nest egg.

Another benefit is that the Thrift Savings Plan keeps its value after you leave federal service.

Should you leave government service before retirement time, your TSP benefits can continue to grow. You'll probably receive more Social Security credits wherever you work next. Also, you may be able to transfer your Thrift Savings Plan account balance to your new employers' qualified pension plan or your individual retirement account (IRA).

If you continue to work under FERS, you have much more control over your retirement benefits. For instance, you decide how much of your salary—if any of it—to put into the Thrift Savings Plan. You also choose where your money will be invested.

Here is a brief review of the differences in the three funds:

The G Fund consists of investments in U.S. Treasury securities.

The C Fund is invested primarily in a commingled stock index fund. A commingled fund is one in which the assets of many plans are combined and invested together.

The F Fund is a commingled bond index fund including government and corporate bonds. The investment fund will be evaluated and readjusted periodically.

There are advantages and disadvantages to each of the funds.

G Fund. There is no investment risk in the G Fund since all Treasury securities are backed by the full faith and credit of the U.S. government. The disadvantage is that the lack of risk means the earnings usually will be lower than those for the other two funds.

C Fund. Gives participants the opportunity to diversify their investments and participate broadly in the U.S. stock market. Investing in a stock index fund provides the opportunity to earn the relatively high returns sometimes available through stock ownership while lessening the effect that poor performance of an individual stock or industry will have on overall investment performance. The disadvantage is that the value of stocks in the fund can decline sharply with unfavorable changes in economic conditions. Depending on the magnitude of the decline, the total return on the C Fund could be negative, resulting in a loss.

F Fund. Consists of a large number of securities selected to produce a fund that represents the various types of Treasury, corporate and agency notes and bonds—including mortgage-backed securities as of January 1991.

The asset manager currently holds more than 500 securities including corporate investment grade securities and obligations of such agencies as the Federal Home Loan Bank System, Federal Farm Credit Bank System, and the Federal National Mortgage Association.

The risks associated with the F Fund are credit risk and market risk. Credit risk is the risk that an issuer of a fixed income security such as a bond will fail to make a payment of interest or principal of the bond backing the investment. Market risk is the danger that the value of the underlying investment may fluctuate from time to time.

Thus, while there is a potential for higher earnings with the F Fund than with the G Fund, there is also a slightly greater risk of loss.

Since there is no assurance that past pattern of return will be continued in the future, you must decide which investment mix is appropriate for you and what level of risk you are willing to tolerate.

LOAN OPTIONS

There are certain conditions under which you may borrow from your TSP account. The loan may be used for one of four purposes:

- purchase of a primary residence,
- educational expenses,
- medical expenses, or
- financial hardship.

You must submit documentation to qualify for a loan in any of the categories.

The minimum amount of a loan is $1,000. The maximum depends on the amount you have in your account. You also must meet an earnings test to show that you can make loan repayments through payroll deduction.

The interest rate will be the G Fund rate at the time the terms of your loan are established. The rate will remain the same for the life of the loan. The interest you pay on the loan will go back into your TSP account. It will take about two months to get a loan approved.

You can repay the loan in full at any time without penalty.

If you leave government employment or retire before the loan is paid off, you **must** repay the loan in full including outstanding interest to the date of repayment. Delay in repaying your loan could delay processing of an application to withdraw the rest of your account.

If you do not repay the loan, the Thrift Investment Board will declare a distribution in the amount of the unpaid loan and any unpaid interest. The distribution will be subject to federal income tax. You may also be subject to the 10 percent IRS early withdrawal tax on this distribution. Once the distribution has been declared you cannot repay the loan and move the loan amount back into deferred tax status.

The documentation requirements for residential, medical and educational loans are detailed in the "Thrift Savings Loan Program" booklet. A supplement to the booklet explains the limitations on financial hardship loans. Both the booklet and the supplement are available from your personnel office.

If you are a CSRS participant your spouse will be notified when you apply for a loan from your account or seek to make a withdrawal when you separate or retire.

FERS participants must obtain the written consent of their current spouse before they may receive a loan from the plan. If you are a married FERS participant when you retire, you and your spouse must sign a joint waiver if you choose a withdrawal method other than a joint life annuity with your spouse with 50 percent survivor benefit, level payments, and no cash refund feature.

Former spouses must be notified when a CSRS or FERS participant who is not eligible for retirement (because of having less than five years of service) transfers his or her Plan account to an IRA or other eligible retirement plan. Further details are contained in the TSP Fact Sheet entitled "The Thrift Savings Plan and IRAs" available from your personnel office.

Your right to make tax-deferred deductions in an IRA depends upon your income and the rules established by the IRS, not upon your participation in the thrift plans.

There are many ramifications to selecting a thrift plan. Each eventually comes down to your personal financial situation and anticipated future needs. Armed with the general information presented in this chapter you should be able to discuss your choices with your retirement counselor and get specific answers dealing with your own situation.

For those now eligible to retire, you may still benefit from the liberalized savings plan.

Note: Although retirees may no longer contribute to TSP, they may take advantage of unrestricted interfund transfers and continued investment until their account is closed.

If you could retire now but are not sure you want to, it will be well worth your time to check out the plan in which you are eligible to participate. Even a couple of years of such savings could make a nice addition to your retirement nest egg.

The Federal Retirement Thrift Investment Board in July 1990

announced a rules change in the policy on interfund transfers of investments. The new rule allows TSP participants to make an interfund transfer in any month up to a limit of four transfers a year.

WITHDRAWAL OF TSP ACCOUNTS

How employees receive their accounts depends upon their status at separation. Employees who retire from the government who are eligible for an immediate annuity may receive their TSP accounts in a lump-sum, in substantially equal monthly payments for a designated period, as an annuity, by transferring their account balances to Individual Retirement Accounts (IRA) or another eligible retirement plan, or by deferring the decision to a later date.

Employees separating from the government who are eligible for a deferred benefit from their basic retirement plan may receive a lump-sum payment or substantially equal payments beginning at the date they reach retirement age, take an immediate annuity (selecting from among the available options), defer their decisions to a later date, or transfer the balance to an IRA or other eligible retirement plan.

For FERS-covered employees, choosing options other than the annuity requires spousal consent, while spouses of CSRS employees will be notified of the election. The board will comply with any valid court order that awards a portion of an individual's retirement benefits to a former or separated spouse, or that enforces payment of child support or alimony. Such an order might require a withdrawal option different than the retiree might desire.

Employees separating from service without title to either immediate or deferred benefit in the basic plan must transfer the balance of their account to an IRA or other eligible retirement plan.

A publication from the Thrift Board available at personnel offices, *Withdrawing Your TSP Account Balance*, more fully explains the options and procedures. Financial advisers also should be consulted regarding the tax and other implications of the various options. These vary from individual to individual and may change over time as tax laws and rules are revised.

TYPES OF WITHDRAWAL ELECTIONS

Lump-Sum or Substantially Equal Payments — The money may be taken out as one sum or on a schedule of regular payments — for example, payments for 5 years or 10 years, or a monthly payment amount until the account is depleted. While payments are being made, the balance must be in the G fund and continues to accrue earnings. The minimum monthly payment under this option is $25. Both the lump-sum and spread out payments are ordinarily taxable income to the retiree in the year in which they are paid. In addition, those retiring on other than disability retirement before the year in which they reach age 55 will be subject to the 10 percent early withdrawal penalty tax on all amounts received before becoming age 59 ½.

IRA Rollover — Transferring the money to an IRA or other qualified pension defers payment of taxes until a time when the recipient likely is in a lower income tax bracket. There is no tax at the time of transfer; however, federal income taxes must be paid on the funds as they are drawn out, according to IRA rules.

You may not transfer any IRA money into the TSP account, however. Nor may you roll over TSP money into the IRA of a spouse. On your death, however, your spouse may be able to deposit a lump-sum payment from your TSP account into his or her own IRA account. A financial consultant should be contacted at that time for guidance on this issue.

Annuities — In this option the plan purchases a life annuity for the employee with his or her account balance. A life annuity is a guaranteed monthly payment for life with or without survivor benefits.

Upon separation, an employee may choose among various annuity forms as long as he or she has at least $3,500 in his or her TSP account. There is a single life annuity that either pays a fixed monthly amount for the duration of the employee's life or a monthly benefit that may change each year of the employee's life based on the Consumer Price Index. If the increasing benefit is chosen, the starting annuity will be reduced to compensate for the subsequent increases.

An optional survivor benefit can equal either 50 percent or 100 percent of the employee's annuity; however, the spouse must consent to any option other than the 50 percent survivor annuity with level payments and no cash refund. In either case, the employee's annuity is reduced based on the spouse's age. Like the single life annuity, the annuity with a spouse benefit can have fixed or increasing monthly payments.

Employees can also choose an annuity with a survivor benefit payable to one who has an insurable interest in the employee.

Employees may also choose two other features, both of which reduce monthly annuity payments. Under the "ten-year certain" feature, an employee and his or her beneficiaries can be guaranteed that the benefit will be paid for at least 10 years regardless of date of death. This feature is available with the single life annuity option only. The "cash refund" feature guarantees payment to a beneficiary in the amount of the account balance used to purchase the annuity minus actual annuity payments if the employee dies before the value of the original account balance is exhausted. Normally, when the employee dies no further payments are made even if death occurs shortly after annuity payments begin.

Annuity payments are taxable when they are made. The 1990 law exempts the purchase of a TSP annuity from state and local premium taxes. Some jurisdictions had imposed a premium tax, ranging from one half of 1 percent to 2 percent.

Deferring the Choice — Those eligible for retirement benefits when leaving government service generally can leave the money in the plan untouched for several months, if not years, until certain deadlines that are explained in the *Withdrawing Your TSP Account Balance* booklet are met. An annuity automatically will be purchased for those who do not make a withdrawal choice by their deadline.

Those leaving government service at age 70 1/2 or older cannot leave all their money in the plan. IRS rules require certain minimum distributions in this situation.

Survivor Benefits — Upon death in service, the balance in the TSP account will be distributed to designated beneficiaries. If death occurs after leaving service, the beneficiary or a third party acting for the beneficiary must apply for the balance with the Board. For those who have selected a TSP annuity, benefits will be provided according to the selection made — unless death occurs before the annuity actually is purchased, in which case the balance will be distributed as in the other situations.

Other Withdrawal Rules — You generally are entitled to 100 percent of your contributions and the money earned on them. The same is generally true of the matching contributions made by your agency if you are a FERS employee. The only money in question is the 1 percent agency automatic contribution for FERS employees. If you leave government service before completing three years of service, you forfeit that contribution. After three years you are fully vested in all of the money in your account.

The law provides that a separated participant may receive an account balance of $3,500 or less in a single lump-sum payment unless a different withdrawal option is selected. Failure by the participant with an account balance of $3,500 or less to elect one of the options explained above will result in automatic return of all investments — a "cashout."

EXAMPLES OF ANNUITY AMOUNTS

An employee's age, the amount in the TSP account, the annuity option chosen, the level of market interest rates at the time the annuity begins, and any additional features added affect the amount of the monthly annuity. In general, the single life only annuity option will pay the largest monthly benefit; a

APPROXIMATE MONTHLY ANNUITY PAYMENTS PER $1,000 OF PLAN BALANCE

	Single Life Annuities	Joint Life Annuities		
		10 Years	100%	50%
	Life	Certain	Spouse	Spouse
Age	Only	& Life	Same age	Same age
45	$ 7.59	$ 7.51	$ 7.03	$ 7.48
50	$ 7.93	$ 7.80	$ 7.19	$ 7.79
55	$ 8.38	$ 8.16	$ 7.42	$ 8.20
60	$ 8.97	$ 8.62	$ 7.76	$ 8.76
65	$ 9.81	$ 9.21	$ 8.25	$ 9.54
70	$11.05	$ 9.96	$ 9.00	$10.71

joint and 100 percent survivor annuity with annual increases and a cash refund will pay the smallest monthly benefit.

An annuity will be purchased from a private insurance carrier 30 days before payment is to start. The thrift board has estimated the above annuity rates assuming an interest rate of 8 percent.

STARTING DATES

Under the old law there was some confusion over the distinction between the date on which an annuity is purchased and the date on which the annuity payments actually begin. It was necessary that the new law make clear the difference since the date triggers certain rights, responsibilities and duties on the part of the participant, the Board and the annuity vendor.

The new law clarifies that those rights, responsibilities and duties transfer on the date the annuity is purchased for the participant.

THRIFT SAVINGS PLAN (TSP)

Provision	Civil Service Retirement System (CSRS)	Federal Employees Retirement System (FERS)
Eligibility	Every 6 mos. employees have an open season to begin or change contributions. Newly hired employees may join at the 2nd open season (6-12 mos. after hire.) All can make interfund transfer 4 times per year	Same as CSRS
Contributions:		
by employees	Employees may contribute up to 5% of pay, with no employer match	Employees may contribute up to 10% of pay
by agencies	N/A	Agency automatically contributes amount equal to 1% of pay into each employee's account Agency also matches employee contributions: 1st 3% of pay = $1 per $1; next 2% of pay = $0.50 per $1
Vesting	Full and immediate vesting	Full and immediate vesting of all except the 1% automatic agency contribution. This automatic contribution becomes vested at 3 yrs. of service for career civil servants, 2 yrs. of service for non-career senor executive service and political (schedule C) appointees, Members and congressional staff

Provision	Civil Service Retirement System (CSRS)	Federal Employees Retirement System (FERS)
Investments:		
1. Employee may elect to invest own account in:	G Fund: special government securities	Same as CSRS
	F Fund: Bond index fund consisting of US. Treasury, corporate, and federally-sponsored agency notes and bonds and mortgage-backed securities	
	C Fund: a stock index fund (invested in proportion to a diversified common stock portfolio designed to replicate Standard & Poor's 500 stock index).	

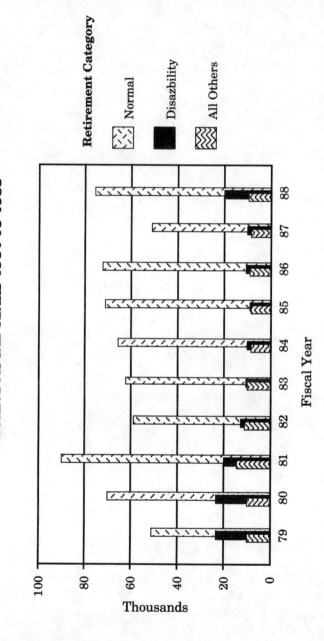

EMPLOYEE ANNUITANTS ADDED TO THE RETIREMENT ROLL DURING FISCAL YEARS 1984 TO 1988

Retirement Category

- Normal
- Disazbility
- All Others

Thousands

Fiscal Year

Source: Annuity Roll

CHAPTER 10

WHAT IF THE CHECK ISN'T IN THE MAIL?

The agencies responsible for sending your checks are prompt and efficient. Once your entitlement has been established your checks will come on a regular schedule. Annuities based on federal or postal service are delivered on the first business day of every month. Social Security benefits are scheduled for delivery on the third of each month.

You should have no reason to contact either OPM or the Social Security Administration unless there is a change in your status or you fail to receive your check on the scheduled date. The following rules must be followed if you do not receive your check. We will deal first with annuity checks.

Some reasons why you might not get your annuity check on time include:

- You moved and didn't report your new address to OPM in time to correct the address before the next scheduled check.

- You received a notice that your annuity check was suspended for failure to reply to official correspondence.

- You began receiving benefits from the Office of Workers' Compensation.

What should you do if the check does not arrive? If you are receiving the checks at your home address, wait five work days because the mail may have been delayed. If no check is received within that time, write to the Office of Personnel Management, Attn: Check Loss, P.O. Box 7815, Washington, D.C. 20044.

Information you should enclose includes notification that the check has not been received, the date you expected to receive the check, the address at which you expected to receive the check and your annuity claim number. (That is the CSA number assigned to you after you retired). At the end of your letter print your name and address and sign the letter. It is important that you sign the letter since OPM can't take any action without your signature.

If you are having your annuity check sent directly to a financial institution and are notified that the check has not been received, you still must initiate the tracer action. Write the letter as described above and get an officer from the financial institution to confirm that the scheduled check has not been received. The signature of an officer of the financial institution must be included with your letter.

Another time you would have to contact OPM would be if there is a change in your mailing address. You should report your new address to the Office of Personnel Management, Change of Address Section, P.O. Box 686, Washington, D.C. 20044.

You can make the change by:

- Using the change of address form provided by OPM.
- Using the form provided on the back of the envelope in which you receive your monthly annuity check, or,
- Use a postal card or letter on which you print the following information:

  your name and date of birth.

  your annuity claim number (CSA number).

  your old address. Mark this clearly as the old address and be sure to include the ZIP Code. Clearly identify the new address.

Whatever form of notification you use, be sure to include your signature, as checks cannot be sent to the new address without a signed authorization from you.

Even if you are receiving your checks on schedule, there are some circumstances under which you might have problems cashing your check.

Suppose that, because of illness, you are unable to endorse your check. If you are mentally competent but physically unable to write your name, you or a person acting in your behalf should ask your bank what you must do to deposit or cash your check. If the illness continues, you should have the checks sent to the bank each month through the direct deposit program. This is one more reason why direct deposit is a good idea.

If you become mentally incapacitated to the point where you cannot take care of your own affairs, your check should not be signed, cashed or deposited by anyone else. Instead, a family member or other person acting in your behalf should return the check to the Director, Disbursing Center, U.S. Treasury Department, P. O. Box 8670, Chicago, Illinois, 60680 with an explanation.

In addition, the person acting in your behalf should notify the Office of Personnel Management, P.O. Box 200, Boyers, PA 16020, being sure to provide your full name and CSA number. OPM then will send instructions to the person who wrote in your behalf and explain how to have annuity payments continued by authorizing payment to a court appointed guardian or representative payee.

SOCIAL SECURITY

What to do if your Social Security check does not arrive on time depends on how you are receiving your check. If it is mailed directly to you it should arrive by the 3rd of the month. If it doesn't, wait three working days. If it is still not received, call the Social Security Help Line at 1-800-2345 SSA and report the loss.

A tracer will be initiated by the SSA office through the Postal Service. If the check still cannot be found, a replacement check will be issued. It usually takes about 30 days before the replacement check can be issued.

There are a number of reasons why your check may not have been received:

- It may have been lost in the mail. Sometimes the carrier delivers the check to the wrong address. Letters and checks occasionally get stuck in the bottom of a mail sack and may not be discovered until the sack is reused. This could be several weeks.

- It may have been taken from your mailbox by a thief. People who steal checks prey on the elderly, particularly on those who have the checks sent to their homes. By observing you a few days the thief knows when your checks come, how long they are in your box before they are picked up, and how long it will be before you cash the check.

The best way to protect yourself is to have the check sent directly to your bank or other financial institution.

• If you already use direct deposit your bank should be sending you a notification of receipt of your check and posting it to your account. If you do not receive such a notice, check first with the bank. They may be behind in their postings. If they say they have not received the check, ask them the procedures they follow in tracing lost checks. If you don't get a satisfactory answer, go back to the SSA Help Line.

If you report a check as lost or stolen, and later receive the check, you can go ahead and cash it. If, however, you later receive a replacement check, that one goes back to the SSA. If you fail to return it, they will catch up with you eventually and deduct it from your future checks.

If, because of illness or incapacitation, you are unable to sign your checks, the SSA will make arrangements to have the checks sent to a "representative payee" who will be empowered to cash or deposit them for you.

In summary, save yourself some headaches. Have your checks sent to a bank or credit union and you won't have to keep an eye on your mailbox.

One other point. The SSA will notify you whenever there is a change of benefits. They will tell you how much you are allowed to earn before you lose part of your Social Security payment. They also want you to notify them of any reason why there should be a change in your benefits, such as earnings beyond the allowable limits, the onset of a disability or changes in your family status. (See chapter 6.)

Whenever you have contact with the SSA be sure to include your Social Security number. With it you get instant answers. Without it you just invite delays.

CHAPTER 11
POST-RETIREMENT EMPLOYMENT

Since this book is designed for people who are eligible to retire, we have to assume that one of your goals is to stop working full-time. If you are considering taking another full-time job after leaving federal or postal service, you should consider the advantages of delaying your retirement. Such a delay would allow you to gain more service time, thereby increasing your retirement benefits.

If you do not plan to take a full-time job when you retire, there are many reasons why you might want to consider a part-time job.

You might want to raise some extra money for a boat, a new car or a nice, long vacation. If nothing else, you might be bored with all that extra leisure time.

Taking a part-time job will not affect your annuity payments. (However, if you are on disability retirement, your outside income from wages or self-employment or both may not exceed 80 percent of the current salary of the position you retired from.) It could, however, affect your Social Security payments if you are also getting benefits from that system. Social Security rules limit the amount of money you can earn before you lose part of the benefits you are now collecting. The amount you are allowed to earn changes each year and increases with age. Your local Social Security office will give you a rundown of the restrictions over the phone. You can call them toll-free at 1-800-2345-SSA. (See chapter 6 for details).

If you are planning to work as a consultant or for a contractor dealing with the federal government, a new set of rules comes in to play. They are long and involved and read like the small print on an insurance policy.

Basically they restrict you from working in retirement on any dealings with the federal agency for which you formerly worked. Most of the restrictions apply for one or two years after you leave your government job.

The restrictions are most strict on those who held high level management or policy-making positions in the agency from which they retired.

The two main restrictions are:

- There is a permanent ban on switching sides which is applicable to key government employees. This means a former government employee may not serve as another party's representative to the government in matters in which he or she participated substantially while in government.

- There is a two-year post-employment ban applicable to all employees. This provision is basically the same as the first with two exceptions. First, it only applies for two years. Second, it covers a broader range of matters by encompassing all specific matters which were actually pending under the former employee's "official responsibilities" during his or her last year of service.

Questions may be referred to the Office of Government Ethics, Suite 500, 1201 New York Ave. N.W., Washington, D.C. 20005. Phone (202) 523-5757.

That takes care of the restrictions applying to contacts with your former agency after you retire. After that the field is wide open and your quest for employment need be limited only by your imagination and qualifications.

Among the factors you will want to consider will be the reasons you decided to work at all after retirement. If you plan to work because you will need to supplement your retirement income, then you will want a job that pays a decent wage.

For most retirees this will require using many of the skills you used in your government job. This probably will involve working either as a consultant or for some firm to which your skill as well as your knowledge of government procedures will be of value.

Look back at the last few jobs you have held. Pick out the elements of the job that gave you the most pleasure. Then, translate those elements into the needs of the non-government job market.

As just one example, suppose your government job involved the loading of ships. Let's say you enjoyed most calculating the amount of cargo that each ship could carry. How would that translate into a non-government job? Easily. The skills required in calculating the amount of cargo a ship could hold are the same skills you would use in calculating cargo capacity for airlines, warehouses, moving companies and in many other businesses.

The main point is to look at your work history in terms of skills you had to use to do the job rather than in what the specific job was called.

If you don't really want a full-time job. There's a world of opportunity waiting for part-time employees.

There are jobs you can do at home and jobs for which you will have to go outside the home. Look for opportunities in the classified ads in the area in which you plan to settle.

Here are a few ideas on the kind of job you might want to consider. Teaching is a great field. If you have a background in education or a degree in education, along with a strong background in your career field, many schools would like to talk with you. What we are considering here is a position in which you would teach maybe one class for a few hours a couple of nights a week. You will have a definite advantage in applying for a job of this type since you will not be looking for permanent status or tenure benefits. Thus, you would not be competing with members of the full-time faculty and would be no threat to their jobs.

If you like the idea of teaching but lack the education degree, there still are many opportunities open to you. Many counties run adult education programs in which courses are offered on a non-credit basis. They are more interested in what job skills you can teach than they are in the degrees you hold. You could teach classes in everything from art to zoo-keeping.

Such jobs are found by looking at the catalog of courses already offered. This will give you an idea of the subject matter in which they are interested and you could plan a related course. If you do not find a course you would like to teach, create one of your own. Look at your civil service or postal specialty. If you were in law enforcement, for instance, you could translate your experience into a course on security programs. If you were in the area of forestry or agriculture you could create a course on home gardens, truck gardens or similar ventures. If you have the ability to write a whole world is open to you in the free-lance writing field.

Suppose all of this seems too technical or looks like too much work. What if all you want is a chance to get out of the house and earn a few extra bucks. Let's look at a few part-time jobs that are not too demanding but are rewarding.

If you want a white collar job try your local bank. Banks are constantly looking for part-time tellers. They know that retired workers have a developed work ethic and are quick to pick up on instructions. Look around the next time you go to the bank. You'll probably see a number of "silver-haired" silver counters (tellers). Banks have other part-time jobs for responsible adults. There are messenger runs to be made to businesses and other banks. You could be a security guard if you like wearing a uniform and meeting new people every day.

Grocery stores are another spot with part-time job opportunities. They want cashiers and other workers who will be available evenings and on Saturdays. If you want or need to work but don't want your friends to know you have taken a part-time job, try to get on as a shelf stacker at an all-night super market. The jobs pay well and you don't run into many of your neighbors shopping in the middle of the night.

Local funeral parlors often hire retired individuals. The jobs involve greeting mourners, opening the doors and directing visitors to the proper area, driving cars or helping direct traffic in the parking lot and cemetery.

If you like working in traffic but prefer dealing with a livelier audience, consider becoming a school crossing guard. This job and that of a school bus driver only commit you for a few hours a day. They get you outside and keep you active—which is another way of saying keep you young.

Car rental agencies frequently employ retired people as drivers. They pick up cars at the airports or railroad terminals and drive them back to the rental agency.

If daredevil driving is your cup of tea, and you are too timid for the racetrack, check out your local pizza parlor and become a delivery person. In the Washington, D.C. area, pizza shops advertise that delivery jobs pay from $8 to $14 per hour and they are always looking for help.

Do you enjoy working around young people? If you do, the fast food places are waiting for you with open arms. They discovered not too long ago that a dedicated retired worker not only does a good job but provides a good example to younger employees.

Sales jobs are always a challenge. You can do them at home by the telephone or you can go out and knock on doors or work in a department store. They always need help. The opportunities for such jobs are even better in the fall when the college crowd goes back to school and leaves all of those empty spaces.

In many part-time jobs you can set your own hours. The amount you can earn is limited only by the effort you are able to apply.

The opportunities are there even if you have no experience. Many employers, such as real estate firms, will provide training if you are willing to work for them after you are trained.

If these suggestions haven't hit your area of interest, go to your local employment office and check what it has to offer. Let them know if the amount you make is more important to you than the kind of work that you do. Chances are good they can meet your needs in both areas.

If money is not a concern to you, consider some of the volunteer projects discussed elsewhere in the book.

Happy hunting!

CHAPTER 12
TO YOUR HEALTH

You probably will hear that toast many times during the last few weeks before you retire. While this toast brings with it a wealth of good wishes, it also carries a warning as you leave your active work schedule—don't neglect diet and exercise as you develop your new life style.

Few retirees realize the amount of exercise they get even in a sedentary job. There are trips up and down stairs to contact other offices. They are many runs over to the copy machine or the coffee maker, the water fountain and the restroom. Lunch time offers a chance to take a short walk to relieve tension.

Many agencies are equipped with fitness centers run on a schedule to allow maximum participation. If you have been using such a center you may notice a major difference in how you feel as you settle into a slower lifestyle. Your muscles get flabby, you probably eat more junk food, and pass up the daily walk for a snooze in the hammock. When I retired I was given a hammock. A stationery bicycle would have been a healthier choice.

Will you be able to stay trim and healthy in retirement? Absolutely! Absolutely, that is if you are eating sensibly and exercising on a regular basis. Both your exercise and your diet should be under the direction of a health professional. Seek guidance from your family doctor, a dietitian in his or her office, or some of the physical fitness specialists at your local gym.

If you find you have to lose weight—and most of us do— avoid crash diets. They do not work and they can have harmful side effects.

Don't expect to lose a lot of weight in a short time. It probably took you a few years to add those extra pounds, one at a time. It is only reasonable to assume that it will be a slow but healthy process as you begin to shed them at the same pace. Remember that any diet that causes rapid weight loss will only result in a fast weight gain once you leave the diet.

If you have a high cholesterol level, suffer from high blood pressure or have a heart problem, you should be on a program that provides a balanced diet and a healthy exercise routine.

Diet meals are not all that bad—they just taste that way. The American Heart Association, among other groups, offers many booklets on the fat content of foods, the calorie value of each and a recommended calorie count for the day.

If snacks are a problem for you, trot out to the produce department and lay in a supply of fresh fruit and vegetables. Carrot snacks may not be a happy substitute for a chocolate bar; but, look what they did for Bugs Bunny. He is over 50 and still gets around like a March Hare.

Check out your local swimming pool. It is another good source of fun and exercise. Swimming, like any other exercise, should be done in moderation. There are no prizes for those who swim one too many laps and end up on the side of the pool having chest pains. Plan a program, set a reasonable goal, and then go a little under that goal each day. As you get in better condition you can raise the goal. Having attainable goals is a key factor in the development of a successful physical fitness program. If you can get your spouse to participate with you, both will benefit.

Many physical therapists recommend alternating a day of strenuous exercise with a day less demanding. This plan gives the sore, aching muscles a chance to recuperate between sessions. This does not mean you should not exercise on the days you are not participating in a formal program. It means you should substitute something else. A good brisk walk is the substitute usually recommended. It will be easier to remember if you tie the walk to some regular daily activity. For instance, you could walk to the grocery store or the post office. On bad weather days you can get good exercise walking around the mall at the shopping centers.

Misery loves company. Enlist a friend to join you in the exercise program. Having company will make the time seem to go faster. Some walkers like to carry a small portable radio and listen to music through an ear plug as they walk. If you take this route, be sure you have at least one ear unplugged so you can hear approaching danger such as a car or emergency vehicle.

If you have a verified cardiac or pulmonary problem you may qualify for a rehabilitation program at a hospital in your area. Some insurance plans cover this type treatment if it is prescribed by your doctor. Programs are of two general types. One is basically a walking program in which participants walk around a marked-off area on a campus or in a school gym. There is a cardiologist and a medical specialist present. Participants are monitored periodically and changes in the routine are prescribed as needed.

A more intensive program is carried on in a hospital cardiac and pulmonary rehabilitation center. All patients are equipped with monitors during their first 12 weeks in the program. Exercise programs are strictly set and a nurse is present to be sure equipment is correctly used. Detailed records and electro-cardiograms are kept throughout the exercise and routines are adjusted as needed. This is by far the most expensive of the programs. While it caters primarily to those who have angina problems or are recovering from a heart attack or open-heart surgery, many of the patients stay on for a modified program when they complete the first 12 weeks.

If you are the shy type and would rather not exercise with a group or trot around the neighborhood in your underwear, you still have many opportunities to exercise.

There are aerobics classes on television. You can also buy videotapes in which models guide you through the routine. If just thinking about exercising makes you tired, you might want to settle for a stationary bicycle. You can sit and peddle while watching your favorite TV show.

Make regular visits to your doctor or dentist a part of your retirement program. He or she will be aware of your medical problems and can often act before a major problem develops.

While our discussion to this point has been limited to physical problems, there is no intention of eliminating concern about mental health.

Many retirees carry excess mental baggage into retirement

with them. They shed the job but still hold on to the tensions and stresses. This makes it hard to adjust to retirement. If you find the transition too difficult, you might want to have a session or two with a mental health professional. Psychiatrists, psychologists and mental therapists all operate under a code of ethics that makes anything told to them a confidential matter. Often having the opportunity to discuss a problem with such a professional removes much of the tension and eases adjustment to retirement.

Finally, avoid situations that introduce strain into your life. Remember that you can't solve all the problems for your children or other family members. They probably will resent your advice and not take it anyway. One of the hardest lessons to learn as we move into our "golden" years is how to cut loose our children. We have spent many years raising them and inculcating them with our values. Now, it is time to let them be on their own. You have taught them how to use their wings, now give them a chance to fly. You can always step in to help in an emergency. But, wait until you are asked for help before you offer it.

You and your children and their children will have a happier relationship if each is allowed to develop his or her own way of life and find solutions to their own problems.

CHAPTER 13
POLITICS IN YOUR FUTURE?

One of the most annoying and disconcerting aspects of retirement, according to many federal and postal annuitants, is the feeling of helplessness as the power elite in Washington D.C. play politics with federal retirement benefits.

As active employees you may not participate in partisan politics, run for office as a member of a political party or engage in a host of other activities that anyone outside of government may without fear of prosecution. A law, the Hatch Act, prevents that. But once retired you may jump in with both feet since the Hatch Act does not apply to government retirees. In fact, federal and postal employee groups look to retirees for help with their political agendas. In effect, retirees often act as their stand-ins when the politics get tough. And tough is just about the only brand of politics practiced in Washington.

It sometimes seems that the only items on the chopping block when it's time to cut Uncle Sam's budget are federal and postal retiree cost-of-living raises and health benefits. In the recent past retiree unrest was not looked upon as a potential danger to vote-hungry politicians but much has changed over the past several years with the emergence of "gray power." Older Americans from every walk of life are banding together to "fight city hall" when their interests are threatened. Their activities have ranged from jumping on the hood of a powerful congressman's automobile (not recommended) to writing letters to their elected representatives and to the White House. One of their most effective methods for increasing political clout, however, has been in organizing themselves into large groups that lobby Congress and meet with senior administration officials.

The most prominent of these groups for federal and postal retirees is the National Association of Retired Federal Employees with chapters in all states and an influential national headquarters located near the White House and Capitol Hill. NARFE—with half a million members—has one of the richest political war chests in the nation and carries a big stick in the halls of Congress. It's lobbyists are among the most effective in the nation's capital year in and year out. (NARFE's address: 1533 New Hampshire Ave., NW, Washington D.C. 20036, phone 202-234-0832.)

While NARFE, federal and postal unions and management groups generally look out for your interests, you can help them and yourselves by staying in touch with the people your voting district and state sent to Congress. You also may contact the President and key committees and subcommittees of Congress that handle federal retiree matters. It's as easy as writing a letter. Keep your letter short, stay on the subject and be polite. Never threaten. Stick to the merits of your case. If you belong to a federal or postal employee or retiree organization, say so. There is strength in numbers and members of Congress are keenly aware of that. Most likely the person answering your letter will be an underpaid and overworked staffer who needs to know quickly what you want. These assistants handle a ton of correspondence for their bosses and the more specific and concise you can be the more effective your letter of support or opposition to legislation, government policies or proposals will be.

Don't think for a moment your correspondence will be ignored. It eventually will be read and if you've stated your case well, or if others have written in on the same subject, elected officials will take notice. After all, it's your vote that's at stake and there is no more precious commodity in the world of politics. Again, you will be augmenting the efforts of employee and retiree organizations who know that they can't do it all themselves.

Following are some of the addresses you'll need to get started.

To write to a member of Congress:

Senators: The Honorable _____, U.S. Senate, Washington D.C. 20510.

House Members: The Honorable _____, House of Representatives, Washington D.C. 20515.

The President: The President, The White House, Washington D.C. 20500.

House Post Office and Civil Service Committee (general federal and postal employee matters) : Room 309 CHOB, Washington D.C. 20515.

Senate Governmental Affairs Committee (general federal and postal employee matters): Room SD-340, Washington D.C. 20510.

House Ways and Means Committee (tax and Social Security matters), Room 1102, LHOB, Washington D.C. 20515.

Senate Finance Committee (Ways and Means' Senate counterpart): Room SD-205, Washington D.C. 20510.

CHAPTER 14
RESOURCES

OPM handles all inquiries from or about civil service annuitants in its offices in Washington, D.C., or Boyers, Pennsylvania, where all retiree records are kept.

All inquiries, whether written or telephoned, should include the name of the former postal or federal employee, the CSA or CSF claim number, date of birth and Social Security number. This information gives OPM quick access to your records and a chance to give you a speedy and accurate answer.

It is possible to get answers over the telephone to questions about your government annuity or Social Security claim. However, it is wise to use this approach only in emergencies. The written correspondence is the best evidence you have of previous action if you have need to question a claim or change in benefits.

There are times when a telephone call gets the job done. One example is the report of the death of an annuitant. Such a report would be made to the Retirement Information Branch (202) 606-0770. Another example would be the reporting of a specific incident of waste, fraud or abuse of civil service annuity benefits. Such information could be reported by phone by calling the "hot line" on: (202) 606-0254.

Written inquiries always are best if the question requires a search of records or seeks to alter records.

Both the annuitant and the government benefit by the use of written communications. The employee has a written record of the answer and the government is able to supply the information at less cost than a lengthy telephone call would entail.

Most written inquiries about civil service annuities should be addressed to the U.S. Office of Personnel Management (OPM), Employee Services and Records Center, Boyers, Pennsylvania

16017. If the question is very complex, it will be referred to the Washington Office along with appropriate documentation.

If you can identify the exact nature of your inquiry you may be able to write directly to the appropriate office and thus get a faster answer. If you are not clear on where the question should be directed, send your inquiry to the Boyers, Pennsylvania office.

There are more than 1,300 Social Security district offices located all over the country. They are listed in telephone directories under "Social Security Administration." The address of your nearest office also can be obtained from your postmaster.

All Social Security district offices have available a wide selection of free pamphlets that may be requested by phone, letter or a visit to the office. Trained personnel at these offices are always glad to discuss questions you have about the program.

There are a number of occasions when it is necessary for persons who are covered by Social Security to contact that agency. If the person eligible for coverage is unable to contact the Social Security office, the contact may be made by someone else.

The Social Security Office needs to be contacted when the person eligible for coverage:

- reaches age 62 or 65 and retires;
- becomes disabled;
- dies; or,
- is still working but will reach age 65 within three months and be eligible for Medicare.

ORGANIZATIONS

Here is a list of federal and postal employee organizations and government offices that you might want to contact with retirement questions:

Federal Employee Unions

AMERICAN FEDERATION OF GOVERNMENT EMPLOY-EES, AFL-CIO. 80 F Street, NW, Washington, D.C. 20001. John Sturdivant, nat. pres.; Allen H. Kaplan, sec.-treas. Phone (202) 737-8700.

NATIONAL AIR TRAFFIC CONTROLLERS ASSOCIATION, NATCA, MEBA-AFL-CIO. Suite 845, 444 North Capitol Street, NW, Washington, D.C. 20001. R. Steve Bell, pres. Phone (202) 347-4572.

NATIONAL ASSOCIATION OF GOVERNMENT EMPLOY- EES. 285 Dorchester Avenue, Boston, MA 02127. Kenneth Lyons, pres. Phone (617) 268-5002.

NATIONAL FEDERATION OF FEDERAL EMPLOYEES. 1016-16th Street, NW, Washington, D.C. 20036. Sheila Velazco, pres.; Alice Bodley, exec. dir. Phone (202) 862-4400.

NATIONAL TREASURY EMPLOYEES UNION. 1730 K Street, NW, Washington, D.C. 20006. Robert M. Tobias, nat. pres.; Bobby Hooten, nat. exec. v-pres. Phone (202) 785-4411.

Postal Employee Unions and Professional Groups

AMERICAN POSTAL WORKERS UNION, AFL-CIO. 1300 L Street, NW, Washington D.C. 20005. Moe Biller, pres.; William Burrus, exec. v.-pres.; Douglas Holbrook, sec.treas.; Patrick J. Nilan, legis. dir.; Tom Neill, dir. of industrial relations; Frank A. Romero, dir. of org.; Kenneth Wilson, clerk director; Thomas Freeman, maintenance director; George N. McKeithen, SDM director; Donald A. Ross, MVS director. Phone (202) 842-4200.

NATIONAL ALLIANCE OF POSTAL AND FEDERAL EM- PLOYEES. 1628 11th Street, NW, Washington, D.C. 20001. James McGee, pres.; Shirley E. Davis, sec. Phone (202) 939-6325.

NATIONAL ASSOCIATION OF LETTER CARRIERS, AFL- CIO. 100 Indiana Avenue, NW, Washington, D.C. 20001. Vincent R. Sombrotto, pres.; Francis J. Conners, exec. v-pres.; Lawrence Hutchins, v-pres.; Richard P. O'Connell, sec.-treas. Phone (202) 393-4695.

NATIONAL ASSOCIATION OF POSTAL SUPERVISORS. 490 L'Enfant Plaza, SW, Suite 3200, Washington D.C. 20024- 2120. Rubin Handelman, pres.; Margarete A. Grant, sec.; Vince Palladino, exec. v-pres.; Bob McLean, editor/legislative counsel. Phone (202) 484-6070.

NATIONAL ASSOCIATION OF POSTMASTERS. 8 Herbert Street, Alexandria, VA 22305-2600. David Hyde, nat. pres.; Jeff

Thompson, exec. dir. Phone (703) 683-9027.

NATIONAL POSTAL MAIL HANDLERS UNION, LIUNA, AFL-CIO. 1 Thomas Circle, #525, NW, Washington, D.C. 20005. Glenn Berrien, nat. pres.; Marion Wright, nat. sec. treas.; Phone (202) 833-9095, FAX (202) 833-0008.

NATIONAL LEAGUE OF POSTMASTERS. 1023 North Royal Street, Alexandria, VA   22314-1569. Armando Olivera, pres. Phone (703) 548-5922.

NATIONAL RURAL LETTER CARRIERS ASSOCIATION. 1448 Duke Street, Alexandria, VA 22314. Vernon H. Meier, pres.; William R. Brown, Jr., vice pres.; Scottie B. Hicks, sec-treas.; Steven R. Smith, dir. of labor rel. Phone (703) 684-5545.

Skilled Trades, Professional, Retirement and Miscellaneous Groups

AFL-CIO PUBLIC EMPLOYEE DEPARTMENT. (Composed of the 33 AFL-CIO federal and other public employee unions). 815 16th Street, NW, Suite 308, Washington, D.C. 20006. Al Bilik, pres., John F. Leyden, sec. treas. Phone (202) 393-2820. Fax (202) 347-1825.

AFL-CIO METAL TRADES DEPARTMENT. 815 16th Street, NW, Washington, D.C. 20006. Paul J. Burnsky, pres. Phone (202) 347-7255.

AFFILIATED GOVERNMENT ORGANIZATIONS. Rhoda A. Ruff, pres.; 160 Beach 137th Street, Belle Harbor, NY 11694.

AIR TRAFFIC CONTROL ASSOCIATION, INC. 2020 North 14th Street, Suite 410, Arlington, VA 22201. Gabriel A. Hartl, pres. Phone (703) 522-5717.

AMERICAN FEDERATION OF STATE, COUNTY AND MUNICIPAL EMPLOYEES. 1625 L. Street, NW, Washington, D.C. 20036. Gerald W. McEntee, pres.; William Lucy, sec-treas. Phone (202) 429-1000.

AMERICAN FEDERATION OF TEACHERS, AFL-CIO. 555 New Jersey Avenue, NW, Washington, D. C. 20001. Albert Shanker, pres.; Robert Porter, sec.-treas.; Gregory Humphrey, director-legis. Phone (202) 879-4400.

AMERICAN FOREIGN SERVICE ASSOCIATION. 2101 E.

Street, NW, Washington, D.C. 20037. Theodore S. Wilkinson, pres. Phone (202) 338-4045.

AMERICAN NURSES' ASSOCIATION. 2420 Pershing Road, Kansas City, MO 64108. Sandra L. Houglan, M.S., RN, dir. labor relations. Phone (816) 474-5720.

ASSOCIATION OF CIVILIAN TECHNICIANS. 12510-B Lake Ridge Drive, Lake Ridge, VA 22192. John T. Hunter, pres. Phone (703) 690-1330.

ASSOCIATION OF FEDERAL INVESTIGATORS. 1612 K Street, NW, Suite 202, Washington, D,C. 20006. David C. Williams, pres. Phone (202) 466-7288.

ASSOCIATION OF GOVERNMENT ACCOUNTANTS. 2200 Mount Vernon Avenue, Alexandria, VA 22301. Richard P. Kusserow, pres. Phone (703) 684-6931.

ASSOCIATION OF PART-TIME PROFESSIONALS. 7700 Leesburg Pike, Suite 216, Falls Church, Va. 22043. Phone (703) 734-7975.

FEDERAL BUREAU OF INVESTIGATION AGENTS ASSOCIATION. P.O. Box 250, New Rochelle, NY 10601. Phone (914) 235-7580. Larry W. Langberg, pres., James T. Burnett, exec. v-pres.

FEDERAL CRIMINAL INVESTIGATORS ASSOCIATION (professional group). Ernest J. Alexander, natl. pres., P.O. Box 691145, San Antonio, Tex. 78269-1145.

FEDERAL FIREFIGHTERS ASSOCIATION. 12225 Interlaaken Drive, SW, Takoma, Wash. 98498, (206) 581-3337

FEDERAL LAW ENFORCEMENT OFFICERS ASSOCIATION. 106 Cedarhurst Avenue, Selden, NY 11784. Robert Van Etten, pres. Phone (201) 667-6387.

FEDERAL MANAGERS ASSOCIATION. 1000 16th Street, NW, Suite 701, Washington, D.C. 20036. Paul E. Trayers, ex. dir. (202) 778-1500.

FEDERALLY EMPLOYED WOMEN. 1400 Eye Street, NW, Suite 425, Washington, D.C. 20005. Jean Christiansen, pres.; Karen Scott, exec. dir. Phone (202) 898-0994.

GOVERNMENT EMPLOYEES RECREATIONAL ASSO-

CIATION, INC. P.O. BOX 422, Great Neck, NY 11022. Milton Blecher, exec. dir. Phones (516) 466-4670, 4673, 4675 & (800) 645-6030 (except NY state).

GRAPHIC COMMUNICATIONS INTERNATIONAL UNION. 1900 L Street, NW, Washington, D.C. 20036. James J. Norton, pres. Phone (202) 462-1400.

INTERNATIONAL ASSOCIATION OF FIRE FIGHTERS. 1750 New York Avenue, NW, Washington, D.C. 20006. Alfred K. Whitehead, pres.; Vincent J. Bollon, sec-treas. Phone (202) 737-8484

INTERNATIONAL ASSOCIATION OF MACHINISTS AND AEROSPACE WORKERS—GOVERNMENT EMPLOYEES DEPARTMENT. 1300 Connecticut Avenue, NW, Washington, D.C. 20036. John F. Meese, natl. coordinator. Phone (202) 857-5235.

INTERNATIONAL BROTHERHOOD OF BOILERMAKERS, IRON SHIP BUILDERS, BLACKSMITHS, FORGERS AND HELPERS. Ande Abbott, dir. Ship Building & Marine Div., 2722 Merrilee Drive, Suite 360, Fairfax, VA 22031. Phone (703) 560-1493.

INTERNATIONAL BROTHERHOOD OF ELECTRICAL WORKERS. 1125 15th Street, NW, Washington, D.C. 20005. Gil Bateman, dir, govt employees dept. Phone (202) 728-6042.

INTERNATIONAL BROTHERHOOD OF FIREMEN AND OILERS. 1100 Circle 75 Parkway, Suite 350, Atlanta, Ga. 30339. James L Walker, Intl. pres., Michael A. Matz, Intl. sec.-treas. Phone (404) 933-9104.

INTERNATIONAL BROTHERHOOD OF TEAMSTERS. 25 Louisiana Avenue, NW, Washington, D.C, 20001. William J. McCarthy, pres.; Weldon L. Mathis, sec-treas. Phone (202) 624-6800.

INTERNATIONAL FEDERATION OF PROFESSIONAL AND TECHNICAL ENGINEERS. 8701 Georgia Avenue, Suite 701, Silver Spring, MD 20910. James E. Sommerhauser, pres. Phone (301) 565-9016.

INTERNATIONAL UNION OF OPERATING ENGINEERS. 1125 17th Street, NW, Washington, D.C. 20036. Frank Hanley., gen. pres. Phone (202) 429-9100.

NATIONAL ASSOCIATION OF AERONAUTICAL EXAMINERS. 1309 North Craven Street, New Bern, NC 28560. Shade M. Barnes, pres., (919) 637-3357, Autovon, 582-7523/7858.

NATIONAL ASSOCIATION AIR TRAFFIC CONTROLLERS. 444 N. Capitol, NW, Washington, D.C. 20001. Phone (202) 347-4572.

NATIONAL ASSOCIATION OF AIR TRAFFIC SPECIALISTS. 4740 Corridor Place, Suite C, Beltsville, MD 20705. Bruce B. Henry, pres. Phone (301) 595-2012.

NATIONAL ASSOCIATION OF ASCS COUNTY OFFICE EMPLOYEES. Wayne Perryman, pres., P.O. Box 318, Lonoke, Ark. 72086. (501) 676-6660. ; Leo Osborne, sec. treas., 740 South Main, Nephi, UT 84648. Phone (801) 623-2182.

NATIONAL ASSOCIATION OF CIVIL SERVICE EMPLOYEES. Exec. ofc. and mailing address: 7185 Navajo Road, Suite C, San Diego, CA 92119. Phone (619) 464-1014, in California (800) 552-8858, elsewhere (800) 854-6533.

NATIONAL ASSOCIATION OF CIVILIAN CONSERVATION CORPS ALUMNI. P.O. Box 16429, 16 Hancock Avenue, St. Louis, Mo 63125-0429. (314) 487-8666.

NATIONAL ASSOCIATION OF FEDERAL INJURED WORKERS. P.O. Box 73578, Puyallup, WA 98373. Phone (206) 848-7442, Wil Clow, dir.

NATIONAL ASSOCIATION OF FEDERAL VETERINARIANS. 1023 15th Street, NW, Suite 300, Washington, D.C. 20005. Dr. Ernest P. Deines, pres.; Dr. Edward L. Menning, exec. v.-pres. Phone (202) 289-6334.

NATIONAL ASSOCIATION OF PLANNERS/ESTIMATORS AND PROGRESSMEN (IFPTE Affiliate). Don Smith, pres., P.O. Box 5112, Bear Creek Station, Belfair, Wash. 98528, (206) 275-5744. Terry Taylor, vice pres., P.O. Box 31921, Jacksonville, Fla. 32230, (904) 772-5629; Howard Wilcox, sec. treas., 3079 Rocky Point Road, NW, Bremerton, WA 98312. Phone (206) 479-4740.

NATIONAL ASSOCIATION OF RETIRED FEDERAL EMPLOYEES. 1533 New Hampshire Avenue, NW, Washington, D.C. 20036. Harold "Hal" Price, pres.; Carolyn Lee Decker, chief, op. off. Phone (202) 234-0832.

NATIONAL AVIONICS SOCIETY, INC. P.O. Box 23055, Richfield, MN 55423. William J. Reed, pres., 8 Palm Desert Dr., West Henrietta, N.Y. 14586. Phone (716) 334-5104. John Gera, sec., P.O. Box 16322, St. Paul, MN 55116. Phone (612) 690-1746.

NATIONAL COUNCIL OF INDUSTRIAL NAVAL AIR STATIONS. Rt. 1 Box 1147-H, Lawtey, FL 32058. Barry K. Adams, pres. Phone (904) 782-1347.

NATIONAL COUNCIL OF JEWISH GOVERNMENT EMPLOYEE ORGANIZATIONS. 45 E. 33rd Street, Suite 604, New York, NY 10016. Louis Weiser, pres. Phone (212) 689-2015.

NATIONAL MARINE ENGINEERS BENEFICIAL ASSOCIATION. C. E. DeFries, natl. pres., 444 North Capitol Street, Suite 800, Washington, DC. 20001, Phone (202) 347-8585.

NATIONAL SOCIETY OF PROFESSIONAL ENGINEERS. 1420 King Street, Alexandria, VA 22314 Donald G. Weinert, exec. dir. Phone (703) 684-2800.

ORGANIZATION OF PROFESSIONAL EMPLOYEES (OPEDA), (Agriculture Dept.) P.O. Box 381, Washington, D.C. 20044. Phone (202) 447-4898.

OVERSEAS EDUCATION ASSOCIATION. 1201 16th Street, NW, Washington, D.C. 20036. Jackie Rollins, pres.; Ronald Austin, exec. dir. & gen. counsel; Sandra Vickstrom, comm. dir.; Joanne Eide, membership dir. & asst. to the pres.; Connie Shanaghan, exec. sec.; Barbara Wright, bookkeeper. Phone (202) 822-7850.

OVERSEAS FEDERATION OF TEACHERS, AFT, AFL/CIO. Dr. Marie SainzFunaro, pres.; Livorno Elementary School, Box 541, APO NY 09019. Phone 0039-586-581047 (Italy). Ernest J. Lehmann, European Director, Verona Elementary School, Box 1276, APO New York 09453. Phone (0039-45) 38943 (Verona, Italy). Mel Cann, vice pres., Vincenza Elem. School, Box 1174, APO N.Y. 09221, phone 0039-444-597196 (Italy)..

PATENT OFFICE PROFESSIONAL ASSOCIATION. P.O. Box 2745, Arlington, VA 22202. Ronald J. Stern, pres. Phone (703) 308-0818.

POLICE ASSOCIATION OF THE DISTRICT OF COLUMBIA. 1441 Pennsylvania Avenue, SE, Washington D.C. 20003. Ralph T. Pfister, pres.; Patrick F. O'Brien, exec. dir. (202) 543-9557.

PROFESSIONAL AIRWAYS SYSTEMS SPECIALISTS. 305 S. Andrews Avenue, Suite 840, Ft. Lauderdale, FL 33301. Howard E. Johannssen, pres. Phone (305) 522-4846.

PROFESSIONAL ENGINEERS IN GOVERNMENT (A division of NSPE). 1420 King Street, Alexandria, VA 22314. Marji Bayers, dir. Phone (703) 684-2833.

PROFESSIONAL MANAGERS ASSOCIATION. Helene Benson, pres. P.O. Box 895, Washington, D.C. 20044. Phone (202) 343-0883.

SERVICE EMPLOYEES INTERNATIONAL UNION (AFL-CIO-CLC). 1313 L. Street, NW, Washington, D.C. 20005. John Sweeney, pres. Phone (202) 898-3200.

SOCIETY OF FEDERAL LABOR RELATIONS PROFESSIONALS. P.O. Box 33013, Washington, D.C. 20033. William Harness, pres. Phone (301) 262-4213.

UNIFORMED SERVICES BENEFIT ASSOCIATION. P.O. Box 418258, Kansas City, MO 64141. Maj. Gen. Larry N. Tibbetts, USAF (Ret.), pres. Phone (800) 821-7912.

UNITED STATES "SKY MARSHAL" ASSOCIATION. 97 Mimosa Lane, Staten Island, NY 10312. Patrick Pacifico, pres. Phone (718) 317-7779.

EDITOR'S NOTE: The above list is as inclusive and factual as possible. If any organization has been omitted or any change of officers or address has occurred, please get in touch with us so that the necessary revisions can be made in time for next year's issue of the *Federal Employees' Almanac*.

Special Groups

In addition to the employee unions, there are a number of organizations whose chief concern is the improvement of personnel management practices in government and protection of the merit system.

AMERICAN ASSOCIATION OF GOVERNMENT EMPLOY-

EES. 8607 Wurzbach, Suite 200, San Antonio, TX 78240; James O. Duncan, exec. dir. Fraternal, benevolent, social and nonprofit. Offers special rates to government workers on various items and services. Phone (512) 694-4950.

AMERICAN LEAGUE OF FEDERAL EMPLOYEES. 1145 19th Street, NW, Suite 201, Washington D.C. 20036. Offers special rates to government employees on various items and services. Phone (202) 862-4911.

AMERICAN SOCIETY FOR PUBLIC ADMINISTRATION. Shirley H. Wester, exec. dir., Suite 500, 1120 "G" Street, NW, Washington, D.C. 20005. Phone (202) 393-7878.

BLACKS IN GOVERNMENT. Marion Bowden, nat. pres. 1820 11th Street, NW, Washington, D.C. 20001. Phone (202) 667-3280.

CIVIL SERVICE EMPLOYEES ADVISORY ASSOCIATION. Bruce A. Rosenberg, pres., 909 Marina Village Parkway, Suite 150, Alameda, CA 94501. Phone (415) 523-2454.

THE FEDERAL BAR ASSOCIATION is composed of present and former federal government attorneys and private practitioners with a federal practice. Current president: Hon. Barry Russell; John G. Blanche, III, exec. staff dir. 1815 H. Street, NW, Suite 408, Washington, D.C. 20006-3697. Phone (202) 638-0252. Fax (202) 638-0252.

FEDERAL EMPLOYEE ASSOCIATIONS/GOVERNMENT EMPLOYEE ASSOCIATION. 1747 Citadel Plaza, San Antonio, TX 78209. Offers special rates to government workers on various items and services. Phone (512) 821-5121.

LEAGUE OF FEDERAL RECREATION ASSOCIATIONS, INC. P.O. Box 70509, Washington, D.C. 20024. A group of over 90 employee recreation associations dedicated to promoting the welfare and morale of government employees in the Washington Metropolitan area. By combining the buying power of all member associations, the LFRA is often able to secure benefits not readily available to a single association. Phone (202) 479-0089.

NATIONAL ASSOCIATION OF FEDERAL EMPLOYEES. 3421 M Street, NW, Suite 343, Washington, D.C. 20007. Phone (214) 526-0314.

INTERNATIONAL PERSONNEL MANAGEMENT ASSO-CIATION. 1617 Duke Street, Alexandria, VA. 22314. John J. Driscoll, pres.; Donald K. Tichenor, exec. dir. Phone (703) 549-7100.

PUBLIC EMPLOYEES ROUNDTABLE. P.O. Box 6184, Ben Franklin Station, Washington, D.C. 20044. G. Jerry Shaw, Chairman. Phone (202) 535-4324. Fax (202) 343-0588.

SENIOR EXECUTIVES ASSOCIATION. P.O. Box 7610, Ben Franklin Station, Washington, D.C. 20044. Carol A. Bonosaro, pres. Phone (202) 535-4328.

Veterans Groups

With more than 50 percent of all of the government's male employees being veterans, the various veterans organizations take a great interest in civil service matters. All of the major veterans organizations have special civil service divisions devoted exclusively to problems of federal workers who are veterans. In the event that problems arise, veterans in the federal service are advised to contact the civil service officers in the veterans organizations to which they belong.

Here are the veterans organizations, their addresses, and the key officials.

AMERICAN EX-PRISONERS OF WAR, 3201 E. Pioneer Parkway, #40, Arlington, TX 76010-5396. Phone (817) 649-2979. Francis W. Agnes, nat. cmndr.; ex. dir. Charles M. Williams, National Capitol Office, 941 N. Capitol Street, #9109, Washington D.C. 20421, (202) 275-1500; Ms. Clydie J. Morgan, nat. adjutant.

AMERICAN LEGION, National Economic Commission. 1608 K Street, NW, Washington, D.C. 20006. Phone (202) 861-2780.

AMVETS. National Hqs. 4647 Forbes Boulevard, Lanham, MD 20706. Robert L. Jones, national executive director. Phone (301) 459-9600, FAX (301) 459-7924.

BLINDED VETERANS ASSOCIATION. 477 H. Street, NW, Washington, D.C. 20001. Ronald L. Miller, PhD., exec. dir. Phone (202) 371-8880.

CATHOLIC WAR VETERANS, USA, INC. 419 North Lee Street, Alexandria, VA 22314. Phone (703) 549-3622

DISABLED AMERICAN VETERANS. 807 Maine Avenue, SW, Washington, D.C. 20024. Charles E. Joeckel Jr., nat. adjt., Washington hqs.; John F. Heilman, nat. legis. dir. Phone (202) 554-3506.

JEWISH WAR VETERANS OF THE USA. 1811 R Street, NW, Washington, D.C. 20009. Phone (202) 265-6280.

NATIONAL ASSOCIATION FOR UNIFORMED SERVICES/ SOCIETY OF MILITARY WIDOWS. 5535 Hempstead Way, Springfield, VA 22151. Maj. Gen. J. C. Pennington, Executive Vice President; Col. Charles Partridge, legis. counsel. Phone (703) 750-1342.

PARALYZED VETERANS OF AMERICA. 801 18th Street, NW, Washington, D.C. 20006. Richard Hoover, exec. dir. Phone (202) 872-1300.

VETERANS OF FOREIGN WARS. 200 Maryland Avenue, NE, Washington, D.C. 20002. Larry W. Rivers, exec. dir. Phone (202) 543-2239.

ADDRESS FOR GENERAL RETIREMENT INQUIRIES

U.S. Office of Personnel Management, Employee Services and Records Center, Boyers, PA 16017

Addresses for Specialized Retirement Functions

Circumstance	Special Address
1. For questions about changing home or check mailing address for those already on the annuity roll. NO CHANGES IN ADDRESSES CAN BE MADE WITHOUT THE WRITTEN AUTHORIZATION OF THE ANNUITANT.	U.S. Office of Personnel Management Change of Address Section — Retirement P.O. Box 686 Washington, D.C. 20044
2. For questions related to student benefits.	U.S. Office of Personnel Management Student Entitlement — Retirement P.O. Box 956 Washington, D.C. 20044
3. For questions related to: a) Marital survey, or b) Income survey for disability annuitants, or c) Waiver of annuity.	U.S. Office of Personnel Management Retirement Inspection Branch P.O.Box 579 Washington, D.C. 20044
4. For questions related to suspected waste, fraud, or abuse in Civil Service annuities.	U.S. Office of Personnel Management Program Integrity — Retirement P.O. Box 7174 Washington, D.C. 20044

Circumstance	*Special Address*
5. For questions involving federal and state income tax. CHANGES IN WITHHOLDING MUST BE IN WRITING.	U.S. Office of Personnel Management Tax Section —Retirement P.O. Box 961 Washington, D.C. 20044
6. For questions involving garnishment or apportionment of civil service retirement annuities, or bankruptcies.	U.S. Office of Personnel Management Court Order Benefits Section — Retirement P.O. Box 17 Washington, D.C. 20044
7. For questions involving health insurance for Civil Service annuitants.	U.S. Office of Personnel Management Health Insurance-Retirement P.O. Box 14172 Washington, D.C. 20044
8. For questions concerning reconsideration of the collection of an overpayment.	U.S. Office of Personnel Management Employee Service and Records Center P.O. Box 107 Boyers, PA 16020
9. For questions concerning the collection of overpayments from former annuitants.	U.S. Office of Personnel Management Reconsideration and Debt Collection — Retirement P.O. Box 300 Washington, D.C. 20044

Circumstance	*Special Address*
10. To report non-receipt of an annuity, lump sum, or refund payment.	U.S. Office of Personnel Management Recertification P.O. Box 7815 Washington, D.C. 20044
11. To report death of annuitant or survivor annuitant.	U.S. Office of Personnel Management Employee Service and Records Center Boyers, PA 16017

MONTHLY ANNUITIES FOR NEW SURVIVOR ANNUITANTS, FISCAL YEARS 1979 TO 1988

Annuitant Spouses

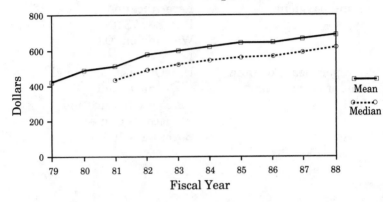

	1979	1980	1981	1982	1983	1984	1985	1986	1987	1988
Mean	$432	$501	$526	$582	$604	$616	$643	$647	$669	$693
Median	NA	NA	$459	$502	$528	$542	$564	$571	$593	$617

Employee Spouses

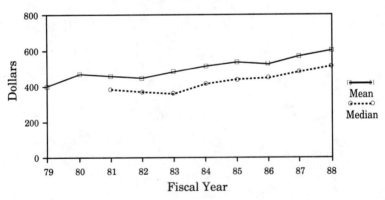

	1979	1980	1981	1982	1983	1984	1985	1986	1987	1988
Mean	$400	$443	$433	$427	$452	$479	$515	$516	$552	$594
Median	NA	NA	$374	$367	$368	$407	$429	$432	$455	$501

Source: Office of Personnel Management

CHAPTER 15
A NEW YARDSTICK

You should begin planning how you are going to spend your retirement at about the same time you begin figuring out how to make the incoming dollars match the outgoing ones once you retire.

Retirement probably will be different than you imagined. If you envisioned spending a lot of time with the people with whom you worked, you probably will be disappointed. Sure, they will be glad to see you when you stop by the office. They may even join you for lunch. But, don't expect your relationship with them to be the same as it was before you retired. Your former co-workers have their own problems and their own concerns. It's not that they like you any less, it is just that you have moved into a different world than the one in which they spend their working hours.

On the positive side, you'll have new interests and you will be able to pursue them at your own pace.

Sit down with your spouse and talk about what the two of you would like to do in retirement. This should be a very open discussion. You may learn more about the interests and dreams of your spouse than you ever knew before.

Let your imagination run rampant as you talk about places you would like to visit and new ventures and adventures you would like to try.

Don't let reality limit your discussion. There is time enough for reality once you have a broad outline of the goals you want to pursue. At that point you may have to make some compromises. For now, dream big.

A large part of turning your dreams into reality is the confidence you have in yourself and the optimistic view that dreams can come true.

Henry Ford said "if you believe you can or if you believe you can't, you are probably right."

You'll need a new yardstick to measure how you want to spend your time and money. You'll be doing many of the same things you did while you were working, but it will be different.

Life becomes like a Whitman's sampler once you retire. You can look at the many paths life offers and go after those you think you will enjoy most. Now, probably for the first time, you have the time and money to do the things you want. You can even do nothing if that is your goal in life.

> *"You have to decide how active a life you want to lead. You may have health problems that limit your mobility. That's why a physical checkup should be in your plans during the last month you are working."*

If you have looked forward to retirement as a time of new adventure and discovery, that's how it will turn out. If you have dreaded the arrival of the time when you would have to leave your job and your friends, you can expect that attitude to be reflected in how you spend your retirement years.

One of the best parts of retirement is the chance you have to do many different things.

Travel is a good example. Before you retired you had to plan your trips on weekends or during a limited vacation period. Now, you are free as the birds. You can take off on Tuesday or Wednesday or whatever day suits your fancy. You will be able to take advantage of all those special fares that require you to travel in mid-week or stay over a weekend in order to qualify. You can visit resort areas at either end of the tourist "season," thereby getting accommodations at much lower cost. What's more, you will probably have smaller crowds than if you went in the middle of the season.

As a "senior citizen" you will be able to avail yourself of the many discounts offered at restaurants and tourist attractions. Some "golden agers" would rather pay full price than admit their age. That's the price of vanity. If it makes you happy then it is worth the extra cost.

It's no secret that we will grow older in retirement. The alternative is not pleasant to contemplate. We can't stop the process, but we sure can delay it.

Each of us has within us a fountain of youth that we carry with us into retirement. It stands ready to flow for us whenever we ask, or to stay dormant if we would rather grow old fast.

The amount of flow you get from the fountain depends on how you prime the pump. Over night you have gone from an active, productive member of the work force to a CSA number, one of millions faced with the task of finding a new lifestyle. Where do you go from here?

You have to decide how active a life you want to lead. You may have health problems that limit your mobility. That's why a physical checkup should be in your plans during the last month you are working.

You may find you will fare better in a warmer or a colder climate. Visit areas in which you think you might live more comfortably. A trip to a possible retirement site does not put you under any obligation. It lets you test the climate and perhaps see parts of the country you have missed before. Since the question of whether to move or not is discussed in Chapter 7, there is no need to consider it further at this point.

You may not want to travel at all. If that is your choice, you should begin to explore the activities and opportunities available in your own area.

You may want to pursue further education, write a book or turn a hobby into a small business. You might want to spend your time in an area where you will be in crowds all of the time or in a secluded mountain hideaway.

If there is a college in your town, visit the campus. Sit on a bench in the park and watch the activity swirling around you. Being with young people makes you feel younger. Joining them in the classroom can be a pleasant experience. There is no age limit on when you can start or go back to college. If you don't have a degree you might want to consider working toward one. If your interest is in just learning about a new subject you can audit a course. This means you can attend the class, listen to the lectures and then go on your way. Since you will not be taking the course for credit, you don't have to do the homework or worry about tests. As an older member of the class, you may be asked to present your viewpoint on the subject matter. Interchanges of this type with the students can be fun as well as educational.

Are you bothered by being asked to speak before a group? If so, hurry over to your nearest Toastmaster Club. You can sit in as a guest for three meetings before being asked to join. There are clubs in most cities. In fact, some cities have dozens of clubs. Through the clubs you get a chance to practice delivering speeches and thinking while on your feet. The butterflies disappear after the first few speeches and then you go on to hone your skills as a speaker. Try it, you'll like it.

Do you have a little gypsy in your soul? Are you willing to try new experiences? Or, are you a stick in the mud?

Spice your life by trying something you haven't done before. Have you ever gone to a baseball, basketball or hockey game? If not, why not? If you have attended games in the better known sports, how about checking out some new ones. Try watching a polo match, a tennis match, a swim meet. You'll meet different kinds of fans at each of them and you have an exciting chance to learn about an activity which you may want to continue watching or even try out for a team.

If you don't care for outdoor sports, how about trying some of the indoor variety—like eating. When you and your spouse go out to dinner do you always go to the same place? It may be good so you keep going back. This week how about trying a different place? Sample Mexican, Italian, Chinese, Indian or Ethiopian, just to name a few. You may enjoy the food and you'll get a language lesson as you try to figure out the menu.

While on the subject of eating, you may find it a good idea to read the menu from the right side to the left instead of the usual arrangement. This lets you know in advance how much "experimenting" your budget will allow.

Looking for another adventure? Check the world of music. Most metropolitan areas offer a wealth of choices. You can sample everything from opera to hard rock, from Broadway musicals to ballet. Just because you may not have been to the theater in years is no reason why you cannot start now. If you are in an area which does not offer this wide a variety of musical programs, you can bring the opera house into your living room. You don't even have to buy the records or discs. You can probably check them out at your library.

How long has it been since you read a book? Have you considered reading a book on a subject that might be new to you? There are books on hobbies, travel, gardening, autobiographies and a ton of "how to" books. Check one out of the library and begin expanding your education. It is fun!

Maybe this would be a good time to consider taking a cruise. You can go to the Caribbean for a few hundred bucks plus air fare. Or, if your budget can stand it, you can take a trip around the world. The two best things about a cruise are the people you meet and the meals. The former gives you a chance for a broader understanding of people from different areas. The latter just gives you a chance to get broader.

If you have the talent, try painting or writing or arts and crafts. If you have the talent but lack ideas on how to exhibit or merchandise your hobby or craft productions, check out local museums, art shops and hobby shows and see what other people are doing. If your skill is in writing, talk with the editor of the local newspaper and see if there is an opportunity for "hometown" writing. If not, get a copy of *Writers' Market* from your library. It lists thousands of places where writing can be sold. Additionally, it provides good tips on how to get publications interested in your work. If you are short on skill or mechanics, consider taking a writing course in an adult education program. If you have considerable skill you could get to teach a writing course. Look at the catalog of courses offered and go from there. You might want to take at least one course to get a feel for the classroom atmosphere and the manner in which courses are presented.

We hope this discussion has aroused your interest and that you are ready to begin exploring the wonderful and exciting world in which we live. There will be days when life gets you down and you wonder if you made a mistake by retiring. That's when you need to get out, look around and count your blessings. Visit a nursing home and talk with people who are confined to wheelchairs. Visit a veterans' hospital and see people who are still paying the price for wars past. Take along some cookies—preferably homemade—and spend a few minutes chatting with those who seem to need comforting. You'll see how much better off you are and life will have a new glow.

The first year of retirement is magnificent. After that, it gets better. Happy retirement!

CHAPTER 16
COMMONLY ASKED QUESTIONS ABOUT RETIREMENT

MEMBERSHIP — RETIREMENT SYSTEMS

Q. *Can a returning employee join CSRS?*

A. Employees who left service with at least 5 years of service subject to CSRS retain rights to reenter Federal employment with CSRS coverage. If the separation was more than one year, the employee will also be covered by Social Security, with CSRS contributions and benefits offset by the taxes and benefits of Social Security coverage during their federal employment.

Q. *Can a returning employee elect FERS?*

A. A rehired employee not automatically covered by FERS has 6 months from the date of rehire to elect FERS coverage.

Q. *How would a returning employee choose between CSRS-Offset and FERS?*

A. Generally, FERS is advantageous for employees who retire in their 60's or later, workers whose careers are spent in the lower-grades, workers inclined to contribute at least 5% of pay to the TSP, and workers expecting to leave their federal jobs years before becoming eligible for retirement benefits. Workers who will probably be better off remaining in CSRS would be ones who become eligible to retire in their mid-fifties and expect to retire soon after becoming eligible, workers who could be involuntarily separated in their early fifties, and workers who can reasonably expect substantial increases in salary within a few years of retirement.

Q. *Can an employee elect no coverage by any retirement system?*

A. No. Employees are automatically covered by one or the other, although some employees and Members of the legislative branch retain rights to be covered only by Social Security.

Q. *Is membership in CSRS retained when an employee of the executive branch is appointed without a break in service to a position in the legislative branch in which retirement coverage is optional?*

A. No. The employee must elect to become a member of CSRS, the same as a person newly appointed to such a position in the legislative branch. Otherwise, the employee would trigger Social Security.

Q. *What is considered a break in service?*

A. Any period of separation that is more than 3 calendar days.

Q. *Must application for optional retirement be made before the employees separate from the service?*

A. No. However, it is advisable to apply in advance of the date scheduled for separation.

CREDIT FOR SERVICE

Q. *How much service is creditable for an employee who is in a leave-without-pay-status?*

A. Generally, not more than six months' leave-without-pay *in any calendar year* is creditable for retirement purposes. For example, if an employee goes on leave-without-pay on January 1 and returns to pay status one year later, he or she receives retirement credit for only six months' service. If an employee goes on leave-without-pay on July 1 and returns to pay status one year later, the entire period will be creditable for retirement purposes.

Q. *Must the service involved be consecutive, or may separate periods of service be counted?*

A. All service is creditable, regardless of breaks in employment.

Q. *In case of death of an employee, may a survivor entitled to annuity benefits make a deposit or redeposit?*

A. Yes.

Q. *How is substitute employment in the postal service credited?*

A. Full credit is given for the time from the date of original appointment, provided the employee was subject to call for duty.

Q. *Can an employee receive retirement credit for military service that is the basis for military retired pay?*

A. Employees who became subject to the Civil Service Retirement Act before October 1, 1982, have the option of either (1) making the deposit for post-1956 military service, or (2) receiving credit and having the annuity recomputed at age 62 to eliminate the post-1956 military service if eligible for Social Security old-age or survivor benefits. An employee who became subject to Civil Service Retirement Act on or after October 1, 1982 will receive credit for the post-1956 military service at time of retirement only if a deposit is made for the military service.

Q. *Can an employee receive retirement credit for military service if he is in receipt of a pension or compensation from the Department of Veterans Affairs?*

A. Yes. An employee may receive civil service retirement credit for military service if he/she is drawing a pension or compensation from VA. However, if the employee is receiving a VA pension or compensation in lieu of military retired or retainer pay, the employee must waive the military retired or retainer pay for civil service annuity purposes in order to receive credit for the military service. A disability retiree may not receive credit for such military service in the computation of annuity, unless the military retired or retainer pay is based on a service-connected disability or Chapter 67 of title 10. This is true even though a waiver of such retired or retainer pay has been initiated.

Q. *Is my unused sick leave credited as service for retirement computation purposes?*

A. Under CSRS, any unused sick leave can be used for service credit in the annuity comptation. Under FERS, sick leave credit is not countable as service credit. Employees switching from CSRS to FERS may use such sick leave credit as they had accumulated at the time their switch to FERS became effective.

DISABILITY BENEFITS

Q. *What constitutes "total disability" for civil service retirement purposes?*

A. Inability of the employee, because of disease or injury, to satisfactorily and efficiently perform the duties or his or her position or any other vacant position at the same grade or pay level within his or her agency and the commuting area for which he or she is qualified for reassignment.

Q. *May disability annuity be based on any disease or injury?*

A. No. It may not be based on a disability of short duration.

Q. *Must the injury or disease be incurred while on duty?*

A. No, if it is so incurred, however, the employee will have a choice between annuity under the Retirement System and benefits under the Federal Employees' Compensation Act, and may choose whichever is to the employee's advantage.

Q. *In case a disability annuitant recovers, what is his or her status?*

A. The annuity is continued temporarily (not to exceed 1 year) to give the annuitant an opportunity to find a position. If he or she is reemployed in the government service within the year, annuity ceases from the date of reemployment. If the annuitant is not so reemployed, the annuity stops at the expiration of the one-year period.

Q. *What happens to a disability annuitant whose earning capacity is restored?*

A. Even if he or she remains totally disabled, an annuitant whose earning capacity is restored before reaching age 60 will have his or her annuity discontinued. If earning capacity is restored, the annuity is continued temporarily (not to exceed 6 months). If the annuitant is reemployed in the government service within the 6-month period, annuity ceases from the date of reemployment. If he or she is not reemployed, the annuity stops at the expiration of the 6-month period.

Q. *Are disability retirees who are 60 years old or older exempt from the 80% of earnings restriction?*

A. Yes.

Q. *Does my Social Security disability benefit affect my retirement plan disability benefit?*

A. An employee eligible for Social Security disability benefits and also entitled to CSRS disability benefits will have the CSRS benefits subtracted from the Social Security benefit. An employee

ployee eligible for FERS disability benefits receives 60% of high-3 pay during the first year of disability, minus any Social Security disability benefits. Thereafter, the FERS beneficiary receives 40% of high-3, minus 60% of any Social Security disability benefits.

Q. *Are disabled retirees under FERS subject to the same 80 percent restored earnings limitations as are applicable under CSRS?*

A. Yes.

SURVIVOR BENEFITS

Q. *May a retiree drawing a civil service annuity also draw a civil service survivor annuity?*

A. Yes.

Q. *Is a child's survivor annuity payable in addition to the widow's or widower's annuity?*

A. Yes. For example, if a deceased employee is survived by a widow and 3 children, all of whom are eligible to receive survivor annuities, this benefit would be paid for all 4 survivors.

Q *If a widow or widower dies, will the children's annuity be increased?*

A. Yes. If the children are still drawing annuity, their payments will be increased as though the employee had not been survived by a spouse, unless a living former spouse is the parent of any of the eligible children.

Q. *If the annuity to one child stops for any reason will the annuity to any remaining children be increased?*

A. When the annuity to any one child stops, the other children's annuities are recomputed as though the one child had never been eligible. In some cases this will increase the annuities to the other eligible children.

Q. *When a child's annuity stops, is the widow's or widower's annuity affected?*

A. No.

Q. *Under what conditions would a lump-sum benefit be payable immediately after the death of an employee?*

A. A lump-sum benefit is payable immediately if the deceased employee had less than 18 months of civilian service, or if the employee had completed 18 months but leaves no widow, widower, former spouse or children who are eligible for a survivor annuity.

Q. *Of what does the immediate lump-sum benefit consist?*

A. The amount paid into the Civil Service Retirement Fund by the employee, plus any accrued interest.

Q. *May a lump-sum benefit be paid if the employee leaves a surviving spouse, former spouse or children who are eligible for a survivor annuity?*

A. No lump-sum benefit may be paid while the surviving spouse, former spouse or children are eligible for a survivor annuity. If when all the survivors' annuities have ended they have received in annuities an amount which totals less than the employee paid into the Civil Service Retirement Fund, plus any accrued interest, the difference would be payable as a lump-sum benefit.

Q. *May an employee or annuitant change or cancel a designation of beneficiary?*

A. Yes. Change or cancellation may be made by executing a new Standard Form 2808.

Q. *Must the husband name his wife as beneficiary on Standard Form 2808 in order that she may be awarded an annuity upon his death?*

A. No. The designation or beneficiary is for the lump-sum benefit only. It has no effect on the widow's right to survivor annuity.

Q. *If an employee leaves the government before becoming eligible for an immediate annuity and opts for a deferred annuity at age 62 and dies before reaching that age, will his or her spouse be eligible for a survivor annuity?*

A. No. The spouse, however, would be entitled to receive the lump sum of the employee's contribution to the retirement fund, including interest.

Q. *Are benefits payable to my surviving spouse from CSRS or FERS affected by Social Security survivor benefits?*

A. A spouse may collect both CSRS and Social Security survivor benefits. FERS survivor benefits are also payable in addition to Social Security; in cases where the Social Security survivor benefit is not payable because the spouse is under age 60, FERS provides special benefits to create a spouse benefit approximate to the benefits payable to similar spouses of deceased workers or retirees under CSRS.

Q. *Wouldn't it be better for my spouse and I to waive the survivor coverage and purchase life insurance from a private insurer?*

A. In a relatively few cases it can make sense to waive survivor coverage and purchase private insurance. Even in those cases, it most likely would be advisable to maintain at least the minimum coverage so that the survivor would retain rights to FEHB coverage in the event of the death of the retiree.

Q. *I've been told that I can purchase a fairly large insurance amount for the difference in my annuity to pay for survivor coverage, even after the cost of retaining the minimum for FEHB rights has been taken into consideration. If, at my death, my spouse invested the insurance payment at reasonable rates wouldn't the payments from the interest on the investment be greater than the survivor annuity?*

A. The details in a comparison of life insurance and federal survivor benefits for specific couples are many, including differences in their respective ages and health, alternative income and investments, and tax liability. Anyone considering this alternative seriously should consult a competent financial advisor with no interest in the outcome. A basic guideline to remember is this: In the simplest sense, an insurance premium is equal to the sum of all the payments made to the people insured, divided by the number of people. A private insurance carrier modifies this basic formula to take into consideration investment return, risk charges, commissions to agents, and profit, none of which is included in the rate you pay for survivor coverage under CSRS and FERS. The remaining cost is paid by the federal government. This subsidized survivor coverage makes it very difficult for a private insurer, at the same cost to the retiree, to match the value of a federal survivor benefit with a life insurance plan.

Q. *Is an annuity, after reductions to provide for survivor benefits, eligible for COLA increases?*

A. Yes. Annual COLAs are applied to the annuity paid to the retiree.

CONTRIBUTIONS AND REFUNDS

Q. *Has the Civil Service salary deduction rate always been 7 percent?*

A. No. The rate was 2 ½ percent from August 1, 1920 to June 30, 1926; 3 ½ percent from July 1, 1926 to June 30, 1942; 5 percent from July 1, 1942 to the day before the first pay period which began after June 30, 1948; 6 percent thereafter to the day before the first pay period in October 1956; 6 ½ percent to the day before the first pay period in January 1970; and 7 percent thereafter. Law enforcement and firefighter personnel are subject to a 7 ½ percent deduction rate effective at the beginning of the first applicable pay period which began after December 31, 1974.

Q. *May a former employee who is eligible for deferred retirement be paid a refund?*

A. Yes, if the former employee files an application with the Office of Personnel Management at least 31 days before annuity payments are scheduled to begin.

Q. *Of what does a refund consist?*

A. It consists of the deductions taken from the employee's salary, any deposits and redeposits paid by the employee, and interest if any is due. It may also include voluntary contributions.

Q. *May the employing agency's retirement contributions be refunded?*

A. No. The agency's contributions are to the retirement fund in general and are not credited to any individual employee.

Q. *How is application for refund made?*

A. Application must be filed on Standard Form 2802. If the employee has been separated for 30 days or less, the application should be filed through the last employing agency. If he or she has been separated for more than 30 days, it may be filed directly with the Office of Personnel Management.

Q. *May an employee withdraw his voluntary contributions account?*

A. Yes. An employee or separated employee may withdraw voluntary contributions and accrued interest at any time before retiring and receiving additional annuity. A separated employee, or one who has transferred to a position not under the retirement system, may withdraw voluntary contributions only and leave regular deductions in the retirement fund. This may be done by marking the application (Standard Form 2802) "Refund Voluntary Contribution Account Only."

Q. *Can annuity or refund payments be attached in order to enforce a judgment or other indebtedness?*

A. Such payments generally are not subject to attachment, levy, garnishment, or other legal process. However, such payments are subject to legal process to enforce a child support, alimony, or separate maintenance obligation. Also, the law requires the Office of Personnel Management, under certain circumstances, to comply with a provision dealing with apportionment of retirement benefits in a state court order, decree, or community property settlement agreement in connection with the divorce, annulment, or legal separation of an annuitant. In such cases, the Office of Personnel Management is required to make payments directly to the former or separated spouse in compliance with court determinations expressly providing for apportionment of retirement benefits.

Q. *Does this bar apply to any indebtedness due the United States?*

A. No. This is another exception to the rule. Amounts payable to the employee in annuity or refund, or due as lump-sum death payment, may be used to settle a claim which the government may have against the individual after due process rights have been extended.

Q. *May an employee voluntarily assign retirement deductions as security for a loan or other purpose?*

A. No.

Q. *May an employee borrow from the retirement fund?*

A. No.

Q. *How are my benefits affected if I take a refund when I leave service before retirement?*

A. Taking a refund of mandatory contributions before becoming eligible for retirement suspends the right to benefits under both CSRS and FERS. However, employees who return to CSRS coverage may recapture this lost service if they repay the withdrawn amount plus interest. The interest owed is the compounded annual interest in effect for each year the refund is outstanding. FERS participants who withdraw their mandatory contributions upon separation before eligibility for an immediate annuity may not recapture the lost service upon reemployment by the federal government.

Q. *May any outstanding refund be repaid at the time of retirement?*

A. Yes, provided all outstanding amounts are repaid before a final determination of annuity amounts is established.

Q. *May any outstanding refund be repaid from the amount of the lump-sum payable when an Alternative Form of Annuity option is selected?*

A. Yes, the outstanding refund and the lump-sum payment can be coordinated and the net difference paid to the employee or to the retirement fund, whichever is owed the net difference.

REEMPLOYMENT OF ANNUITANTS

Q. *May an annuitant be reemployed in the federal government?*

A. Yes. He or she may be reemployed in any position for which qualified.

Q. *What effect will reemployment in the federal government have on annuity payments?*

A. In general, annuity payments and the salaries of returning annuitants may not be combined. Either the salary of the reemployed annuitant will be offset by the annuity amount, or the annuity will be suspended for the period of reemployment, depending upon the type of retirement for which the annuity is paid. After meeting certain conditions, a reemployed annuitant may earn a recomputation of the annuity upon subsequent retirement.

Q. *Will mandatory contributions be deducted from the pay of reemployed annuitants?*

A. Reemployed annuitants who have recovered from disability or who were involuntarily separated, become subject to mandatory deductions under both CSRS and FERS. Other reemployed annuitants whose annuities are subtracted from their pay may elect to have deductions made.

Q. *How are subsequent rights affected by the decision to forego contributions upon reemployment as an annuitant?*

A. A reemployed annuitant electing deductions from pay may have the annuity recomputed if subsequent retirement occurs after one year of reemployment. A reemployed annuitant not electing to have deductions withheld from pay must work five years in order to have a recomputation of annuities made at subsequent retirement. In such cases, the reemployed annuitant will owe payments equal to the outstanding amount of deductions, plus interest computed at the going rate for fund transactions.

TAXATION OF BENEFITS

Q. *Must an annuitant have federal income tax withheld from annuity payments?*

A. Yes, unless the annuitant submits a specific election not to have withholding apply. The Tax Equity and Fiscal Responsibilities Act of 1982 (PL 97-248) requires a standard withholding unless the individual requests no withholding (in writing) or has already filed a withholding form (W4A) in the past.

Q. *Why is my lump-sum payment taxable when I elect an Alternative Form of Annuity? Didn't I pay taxes on my contributions at the time they were deducted from my pay?*

A. Taxes were paid on contributions made to CSRS and FERS at the time service under the systems was performed. However, the lump-sum payable under the Alternative Form of Annuity is treated as a payment made to you of an amount **equal** to your contributions. Thus, the lump-sum is regarded as simply another payment from the program, and is therefore subject to the same tax rules that apply to all plan payments. This has been challenged in federal court, however, and the court may rule on the matter in 1991.

Q. *How are tax liabilities determined on my payments under CSRS and FERS?*

A. The total payments you are expected to receive in your lifetime are assumed to be paid from funds either contributed by you or in your behalf. Your tax liability consists of the annuity funds either contributed by you or your employer that have not before been taxed as income. In other words, you owe taxes on the federal government share of your retirement benefits. Thus, in any payment from CSRS or FERS, that portion of the payment that represents the portion of your expected lifetime benefits paid by the federal government is subject to taxation as untaxed income. Your contributions, upon which you have paid income taxes, are divided by the number of years of your life expectancy, and that amount is available as an annual deduction from your taxable income.

MISCELLANEOUS—CSRS AND FERS

Q. *May a person decline to accept all, or a part of, his or her civil-service annuity?*

A. Yes.

Q. *How is this done?*

A. By signing a waiver and filing it with the Office of Personnel Management. No special form is necessary. The annuitant merely states in writing how much of the annuity he or she waives.

Q. *May the waiver be revoked?*

A. Yes. It may be revoked in writing at any time but only with respect to future payments.

Q. *What recourse has an applicant under the Retirement System if the claim is denied?*

A. Any action the Retirement and Insurance Group takes affecting a person's retirement rights is subject to reconsideration. If an employee or agency feels that the action is improper, a reconsideration may be requested. Requests for reconsideration must be filed directly with the Retirement and Insurance Group, P.O. Box 300, Office of Personnel Management, Washington, DC 20044.

Q. *How are my career contributions treated now that I no longer can receive a lump-sum?*

A. Under the law, your contributions are part of your eligibility criteria. When the law provided for a payment of amounts based upon your contributions, that was not considered an actual payment to you of your contributions, but an initial lump-sum *equal to* your contributions. Your annuity was reduced by a complex actuarial formula so that on average you would receive the same in lifetime benefits whether you elected the lump-sum and reduced benefits or refused the lump-sum and took unreduced benefits. Because of the repeal of the lump-sum provisions, your contribution amounts are no longer relevant to your benefits, unless you meet specific circumstances that require the computation of a lump-sum.

THRIFT SAVINGS PLAN

Q. *Can I contribute to both my TSP account and my IRA?*

A. Yes. Even though you are participating in the thrift savings plan you are still eligible to contribute to your IRA. The following IRS rules apply to IRA contributions:

Anyone with wages can contribute up to $2,000 per year to an IRA and defer taxes on the *earnings. Contributions* to an IRA are fully deductible from income for federal tax purposes only if your adjusted gross income is $25,000 or less per year on a single return or $40,000 or less on a joint return. If your adjusted gross income is between $25,000 and $35,000 on an individual return, or between $40,000 and $50,000 on a joint return, you may still qualify for a partial deduction.

The civil service retirement system (CSRS), the federal employees retirement system (FERS) and equivalent government retirement plans are considered to be retirement plans for purposes of IRA eligibility. Thus, participants in the TSP must abide by the following general rules for federal and postal employees: A federal employee whose compensation is less than the applicable limits referred to above may contribute up to $2,000 per year to an IRA and may also take the total or partial IRA deduction. A federal employee whose compensation exceeds the applicable limits may still contribute up to $2,000 per year to an IRA, but may *not* take the IRA deduction. Your IRA provider can give you additional information about the way IRA rules may apply to your situation.

Q. *Can I use my gross income after my TSP contributions to determine if I am eligible to deduct my IRA contributions?*

A. This question should be referred to your tax adviser. The Thrift Board's informal reading of the federal tax code is that you can use your adjusted gross income (which will not include the amount you contributed to your TSP account) to determine if your income is at or below the applicable limits to qualify for an IRA deduction.

Q. *Can I transfer my IRA into my TSP account?*

A. No. Contributions to TSP accounts can be made only through payroll deductions. The law does not allow the transfer of money into the plan from an IRA or other source.

Q. *If I leave government service can I transfer my TSP account to my IRA?*

A. Yes. Transfers to IRAs from the plan are not subject to the annual limits on IRA contributions. In addition, you do not pay taxes on the money you transfer to your IRA until it is withdrawn. (If you receive your TSP account balance in one year and then roll it over into an IRA within 60 days of receiving it, you will be able to defer paying taxes on it and avoid a possible early withdrawal penalty.)

Q. *Can I transfer any of my TSP contributions into my spouse's IRA?*

A. No. You cannot transfer the money in your TSP account into the IRA of your spouse. Your TSP account is in your name; transferring it into your spouse's account would transfer ownership as well as tax liability and is not permitted. However, death and divorce situations may affect this answer. You may wish to consult with a tax adviser or appropriate taxing authority for guidance on this issue.

Q. *If I leave government service and decide to keep my money in the TSP, can I continue to switch my money among funds?*

A. Yes, provided you have at least five years of government service.

Beginning in 1991, all participants may transfer their balances among the three funds four times a year in any month they choose. Interfund transfer request forms, Form TSP-30, are available from the TSP Inquiry Line (toll call, (504) 255-8777). In addition, when a transfer is executed, the participant will receive a TSP-31, confirming the transfer, accompanied by Form TSP-30 for future transfers. Participants with less than five years of government service must, by law, withdraw the funds in their TSP account.

ABOUT OUR PUBLICATIONS

For nearly five decades the editors of Federal Employees News Digest, Inc., have furnished federal and postal employees with news and information vital to their careers. Where other news sources fail to deliver, the company's family of publications and special reports have succeeded in delivering concise, understandable news concerning federal and postal pay and benefits.

Our reporters go straight to the sources, the administration's top policy-makers, key members of Congress. And they canvas the courts to stay abreast of developments that impact directly on the working lives of employees from the giant Defense Department and U.S. Postal Service to the smallest agencies. But the coverage doesn't stop there. The editors also pay close attention to changes in federal retirement—COLAs, eligibility rules, claims to annuities spouses may have, important judicial rulings, lump-sum annuities, virtually all aspects of retirement.

FEND currently offers three regular publications:

- WEEKLY FEDERAL EMPLOYEES' NEWS DIGEST — This weekly newsletter comes in four pages and is full of short, tightly written items that are the most up-to-the-minute news available on your active and retired federal careers. Use this, if you wish, in conjunction with the Federal Employees' Almanac to stay ahead of the game.

- FEDERAL EMPLOYEES' ALMANAC — Updated annually, the 288-page-plus reference book contains more than 200 subjects, including, pay tables, CSRS and FERS retirement, Social Security, health and life insurance, leave and holidays, injury benefits, labor-management relations, collecting benefits, the U.S. Postal Service's pay and employment policies, veterans benefits and employment preference, key labor and court decisions, lists of top officials, inspectors general and their phone numbers and addresses, travel and relocation allowances, special tax features for federal workers, Medicare, promotions and transfers, whistleblower protections, separation and reinstatement, and much much more.

- YOUR RETIREMENT; HOW TO PREPARE FOR IT/HOW

TO ENJOY IT — The newest of our family. This comprehensive guide helps federal and postal employees orient their thinking about one of the most important decisions they'll even have to make—when and how to retire without making major mistakes that they'll regret as long as they live. How to begin preparations, how to estimate income and deal with "outgo," and what options they have. At nearly 200 pages, the guide fills a huge information void for those who are approaching retirement and those who already have separated and need ideas on how to enjoy themselves in retirement.

For more information on these publications please write to:

Federal Employees' News Digest
P.O. Box 7528
Falls Church VA 22040

Need Another Copy...

...for a friend, co-worker or relative who would benefit from having their own copy of *Your Retirement: How To Prepare For It — How To Enjoy It?* It's easy to do—and makes a great gift idea too!

Just fill out the handy order form below and return it to:

Federal Employees' News Digest
Post Office Box 7528
Falls Church, VA 22040

Order Form

Yes, please send me _____ copy/copies of *Your Retirement: How To Prepare For It — How To Enjoy It* at the low price of $9.95 each (postage and handling included).

Total amount enclosed $_____ .

Name _____

Agency/Firm _____

Address _____

Home   Work   Mail Code

City _____ State _____ Zip Code _____

❏ Visa ❏ MasterCard ❏ Check or Money Order enclosed

Account # _____ Exp. Date _____

Your Signature _____
(Required only if using credit card)

Federal Employees News Digest
P.O. Box 7528
Falls Church, VA 22040

Order Form

Need Another Copy...

...for a friend, co-worker or relative who would benefit from having their own copy of *Your Retirement: How To Prepare For It — How To Enjoy It?* It's easy to do— and makes a great gift idea too!

Just fill out the handy order form below and return it to:

Federal Employees' News Digest
Post Office Box 7528
Falls Church, VA 22040

Order Form

Yes, please send me _____ copy/copies of *Your Retirement: How To Prepare For It — How To Enjoy It* at the low price of $9.95 each (postage and handling included).

Total amount enclosed $ _____.

Name _____

Agency/Firm _____

Address _____

Home   Work   Mail Code

City _____ State _____ Zip Code _____

❑ Visa ❑ MasterCard ❑ Check or Money Order enclosed

Account # _____ Exp. Date _____

Your Signature _____
(Required only if using credit card)